EXPE

THE

SUPERNATURAL

Library of Congress Cataloging-in-Publication Data: 2016

International Standard Book Number:

E-book International Standard Book Number:

While the author has made every effort to provide accurate telephone numbers and Internet addresses at the time of publication, neither the publisher nor the author assumes any responsibility for errors or for changes that occur after publication.

First edition

16 17 18 19 20 — 987654321

Printed in the United States of America

Table of Contents

Introduction

There is a desire built into the human heart for the supernatural. Many people go into the occult because they are drawn to the supernatural and don't know the difference between the deceptive power of Satan and the real power of God. Many movies have messages regarding the supernatural, including superheroes who have some kind of superpower and magical or supernatural events. Books like *Harry Potter* were global bestsellers and made their author not only world-famous but also incredibly rich. How can such a message be so influential and loved by millions of people of all social classes and diverse ages all over the world? It is because of this deep desire for the supernatural world that is built inside the human heart.

Unfortunately, the church at large is not moving in her God-given authority and power. We should be demonstrating the answer to these hungry hearts who are longing for the supernatural the world over. The early church moved in the supernatural power of the Holy Spirit on a daily basis. Today we occasionally see some miracles, and when we do, we get excited because they are so rare. I believe that before Jesus returns, He will have a bride that moves in her God-given power, authority, anointing, and purpose.

We have become so accustomed to living in the natural that most of the time we don't expect the supernatural. In crisis situations, our first reaction, too often, is to look for a natural solution. When we are sick, we reach for the medicine cabinet or run to the doctor—and only when they cannot help us do we go to prayer as a last resort. I believe we have things backward. Our first response in any situation should be to expect a miracle. We should expect miracles on a daily basis.

We should expect not only healings, but everything that belongs to us as sons and daughters of God. I have been longing to live an abundant life, just as Jesus promised to us in His Word, since I was a small child. I have seen thousands of miracles: cancers healed, deaf ears opened, cripples walking, and missing body parts supernaturally re-created by God. I have been transported supernaturally several times from one place to another, quite far away, including once with my car.

When people hear some of the stories which I have experienced, they think that I am someone special, which is totally untrue; in fact, such man-worship is idolatry and greatly displeasing to God. I am just a simple man, hungry for the glory of God to be manifested all over the world and for Jesus to be magnified. Often I have told the Lord that I will never tell another story about any of my experiences because of the wrong perception people can have about me. However, I have come to the persuasion that many of these stories inspire my brothers and sisters in Christ to pursue Jesus and the power of His kingdom in order to glorify His great name.

If you took the Bible and tore out every single page where there is some occurrence of the supernatural, you would only have a fairly thin Bible left afterward. You would have to tear out the very first page, as the whole creation is totally supernatural. The spiritual world exists and is absolutely real, even though we cannot see it with our natural eyes. We must believe in it, ask God to open our spiritual eyes, long for it to manifest in our lives, and by faith bring the supernatural into our natural world daily—if for no other reason than to glorify Jesus and demonstrate to the world that He is alive and well and loves them. We must realize that we are much more accustomed to a natural lifestyle than a supernatural one, which must change.

By no means do I dare think that I have attained to a perfectly supernatural lifestyle. I do not compare my life to that of any other Christian, whether they are well advanced or well behind in their experience of the supernatural. I only compare myself to the standard of the Bible, which shows me that I still have a long way to go in this area. My Jesus said that those who believe in Him would do the same works that He did and greater ones (John 14:12). He raised the dead, multiplied food, healed all those who came to him expecting a miracle, turned water into wine, walked on water, calmed the storm and the waves, and did many more extraordinary and supernatural things. He and His Word alone are my standard. If we are supposed to do greater works than He did, why is the church of Jesus at large not fulfilling that promise? That is the question that we must ask ourselves.

I strive to live a life of the supernatural in order to glorify my Lord Jesus and demonstrate to this world that He is alive and loves them deeply. I say along with the apostle Paul, who declared,

Not that I have already attained, or am already perfected; but I press on, that I may lay hold of that for which Christ Jesus has also laid hold of me.

—PHILIPPIANS 3:12

It is my desire and prayer that this book will challenge you, create a deep longing in your heart for the supernatural, and make you so desperate that you will give up food and sleep in order to "lay hold of that for which Jesus has also laid hold of [you]."

However, I must warn you that I personally don't know anyone who moves regularly in the supernatural power of the kingdom of God who did not have to embrace death. It should be normal for all Christians to embrace death, yet many shy away from it. We must die daily as Paul said (1 Cor. 15:31). We must die to our dreams, desires, fears, pride, selfishness, fear of man, and many more such things. We cannot move in the supernatural power of God and be alive to ourselves. We have to live a life of total surrender, which is a very small price to pay compared to the glory that we will see.

One aspect of dying to self is fasting. We never fast to convince God to do a miracle; Jesus already paid for every miracle we will ever see. We fast for ourselves: to surrender and humble ourselves, to deny our body food, and to use the time—instead of eating—to pray and be in the presence of God. When I add up all the days I have gone hungry in the last 34 years, it is nothing compared to the thousands of miracles I have seen and the countless lives that Jesus touched through me for His glory. If you are not willing to embrace death-to-self, a life of the supernatural will be unreachable for you.

In this book, there are testimonies of miracles at the end of every chapter. I am not the one telling these stories; they are told by the very people who experienced them. They have sent me their testimonies and agreed to have them put in this book. We have the names and locations of all of these people, but chose to only mention them by their first name. They are told to encourage you to believe that our God is a supernatural God. Through these stories, no man shall be glorified; Jesus alone shall be praised and lifted up.

—REINHARD HIRTLER

Chapter 1

God's Desire

When we talk about the supernatural, we have to understand that it is God's desire, far more than it can ever be our desire, to see the supernatural power of God manifested. As it is written in Psalm 105:4–5,

> *Seek the LORD and His strength; seek His face evermore! Remember His marvelous works which He has done, His wonders, and the judgments of His mouth.*

We are told to seek the Lord *and* His strength. I have heard preachers say that we must not seek the power of God, but only His presence. Although that sounds very spiritual, it is not biblical. In the above scripture, we are told to also seek His strength. His strength is His manifested supernatural power.

To *seek* means "to long for" or "to desire." God would never tell us to desire something that He would not want us to have or that would be impossible for us to obtain. He is a good God and a caring Father. What kind of father would tell his children to earnestly ask him for something that he had already decided not to give to them? I am sure you would agree with me that this would be a terrible father. God is a loving Father who will not tease us by telling us to desire something that He plans not give to us.

The Gifts of the Spirit

In 1 Corinthians 12 and 14, the apostle Paul talks about the church as a body and about spiritual gifts. There are nine spiritual gifts mentioned, which include prophecy, speaking in tongues, interpretation of tongues, word of wisdom, word of knowledge, gift of faith, gift of healings, gift of miracles, and discerning of spirits. All of these nine gifts are supernatural manifestations of the power of God which should be expressed regularly through the body of Christ. It is my conviction that these gifts should never be absent in the lives of Christians.

Let us look at what the Bible says in the context of these gifts. In 1 Corinthians 12:31 and 14:1, Paul says the following:

*But earnestly desire the best gifts. And yet I
show you a more excellent way. Pursue love,
and desire spiritual gifts, but especially that
you may prophesy.*

Zēloute, the word in the original Greek translated as "earnestly desire," means "to burn with a fiery zeal" or "to chase after."[1] This does not describe an emotion but an action. In the original grammar, it is written in a way that clearly describes something we *do* and not something we *feel.* Several people have told me that they don't have this burning desire or fiery zeal to pursue spiritual gifts. My response is always the same: "God doesn't expect you to have this emotion, but He surely does expect you to obey His written Word and earnestly pursue these spiritual gifts which are an expression of the supernatural power of God." Since God wrote this in the Bible, we can be sure that it is His desire for us to move in these supernatural gifts.

Why Does God Want to Do Miracles?

That is a very important question, since it deals with the motive and the heart of God. We need to know the reason why God desires to show His supernatural power. To understand this will not only help us to pursue it more actively, but it will also help us begin tapping into the supernatural power of God by faith. As we discover the motives behind God's desire to express His supernatural power, we will also discover something about His character.

I have said many times in meetings that I don't believe that God does miracles. The reaction is always the same. People are always shocked, and in their body language, I can clearly see that they disagree with me; sometimes, they even verbalize it. Once I explain what I mean by that statement, people's hearts are usually filled with excitement about this revelation.

God is not a natural or human being; He is a supernatural being. When a supernatural being does something supernatural—which from our earthly perspective looks like a miracle—it is not a miracle from His perspective; it is just natural for Him. God simply acts according to His nature. Therefore, it is not a miracle for Him, only for us, because we are too bound to the natural.

We must move away from our natural limitations and into the supernatural realm of God.

Every miracle that God has ever done and will ever do can only be described as a miracle from an earthly perspective—but not from a heavenly one. If we can only grasp that miracles are the most natural, normal things for God to do, we would constantly expect them in our daily lives.

If a horse were to talk to us, we would all be shocked and surprised, yet when our friends talk to us, we are not surprised. That is because it is normal and natural for humans to speak and not for horses to do so. The very fact that we are so surprised when God does a miracle shows that we have not yet understood God's true nature which is supernatural. We constantly put Him in our category—in the realm of the natural. I will now discuss some reasons why God wants to do miracles.

God Is Love

Since He is love, He loves us and every human being on the planet equally passionately. Love must be expressed through actions and not only in words. In English, there is a saying which I consider to be very stupid, and that is, "It's the thought that counts." What this expression means is that at times people think about doing something or buying something nice for you, but for some reason do not carry it out. They will then tell you, "I thought about doing it, and it's the thought that counts," meaning that you should be glad that they at least thought about doing it for you.

This year my wife and I will celebrate 30 years of marriage. It has been her desire for me to take some time off and take her to a special place to celebrate this anniversary. I thought a lot about where to go and what to do. Can you imagine what she would feel like if, when our anniversary arrives and she asks me where we are going, I simply say, "Nowhere. But don't worry; I put a lot of thought into it, and it's the thought that counts"? She would not be very excited.

God loves us passionately, and His love must be expressed not only in thoughts, but also in deeds, according to His nature. Throughout the entire Bible, we see that God did miracles as an expression of His love for people. It started right in the beginning with creation. We are told in Genesis 2:9,

> *And out of the ground the LORD God made every tree grow that is pleasant to the sight and good for food.*

Out of nothing, God created thousands of trees that were pleasant to the sight and good for food. This supernatural act of God shows His deep love and generosity toward people. In Genesis 2:16, the Bible says,

> *And the LORD God commanded the man, saying, "Of every tree of the garden you may freely eat."*

God did this miracle of creation out of His great love for people. Why did God give Abraham a son? Remember, Sarah was barren, and Abraham was already old. In the natural, it was impossible for them to have children. God did a miracle, which was motivated by His love. As you study the Bible, you will see that God initiated the conversation with Abraham. We are told in James 2:23 how deeply God loved Abraham:

> *And the Scripture was fulfilled which says, "Abraham believed God, and it was accounted to him for righteousness." And he was called the friend of God.*

Abraham was God's friend. That is a beautiful expression of a loving relationship between two people. God's love motivated Him to give Abraham the miracle of a son.

Why did God supernaturally deliver the people of Israel from slavery? The answer, again, is because He loved them. We are shown in Exodus 3:7–8 that God cared for the people:

> *And the LORD said: "I have surely seen the oppression of My people who are in Egypt, and have heard their cry because of their taskmasters, for I know their sorrows. So I have come down to deliver them out of the hand of the Egyptians, and to bring them up from that land to a good and large land, to a land flowing with milk and honey, to the place of the Canaanites and the Hittites and the Amorites and the Perizzites and the Hivites and the Jebusites."*

God heard their cry, and His heart of love moved Him to act supernaturally on behalf of His people. His promise of a beautiful land flowing with milk and honey, which was supernaturally given to them, was another expression of His love.

We could go on and on as we study the Bible about how God did miracles in order to express His love. Why did God use Joseph to supernaturally provide for His people and save them from the famine? Why did Jesus, as He walked around, heal all the sick that came to Him? We could ask many questions like this, and a part of the answer will always be the same—because He loves people.

Endnote

1. *zéloó*, "earnestly desire," Strong's #2206; http://biblehub.com/greek/2206.htm, accessed 15 September 2016.

Testimony

My name is Renata, and I am 33. I had surgery on my hip bones near the lumbar spine in the USA. My brain then started to *release* the pain memory which I felt during the postoperative period; the doctors call it *phantom pain*. The pain was constant, and it was growing more intense, especially when I walked or stood still. Simple things such as house cleaning, having a shower, or shopping for food would bring me great pain, almost unbearable. For two years, the pain wouldn't stop even for a moment, and there was no treatment in Brazil or abroad. But one day, my husband received a prophetic word in which people prayed for me and I was healed. After that, I was invited to take part into a conference, and, even though I was in a lot of pain, I decided to go. At the end of the preaching, there was a moment when all the church prayed for me, and I took, by faith, the truth that God's faith was put in me when I received Jesus. At this moment, I had a fresh sensation in my back, where there used to be pain. I went back home after the meeting, and I could sleep well, with no pain. I didn't wake up in the middle of the night. I can say that I am totally healed for the glory o

Chapter 2

Further Reasons Why God Wants to Do Miracles

God Loves to Glorify His Name

God has this deep desire in His heart to glorify His own name. The Bible is full of this truth. One of the reasons God does any miracle is to bring glory to Himself. Since miracles glorify God's name and this is a deep desire in His heart, we can be sure that God always wants to do miracles. He especially delights in using weak channels. We have to understand the difference between the channel and the source. The power comes from the *source* and flows *through* the channel. The weaker the channel is the more obvious it will be that the source has to be God, which brings Him all the glory.

It grieves the heart of God when He expresses His supernatural power through human channels—and people then give glory to the person through whom the miracles happen. God does not do miracles so that the people He uses can be elevated or get any of the glory for themselves. He performs miracles to glorify His own great name.

In some of my weakest moments, I have seen the greatest releases of the power of God flowing through me. The apostle Paul had to learn this lesson too; he understood that when he was weak it was so that God's power could be made visible through him. If you study the lives of men and women of God throughout history who have been powerfully used by God in the area of the miraculous, they always had to come first to the death of themselves before they were able to be used by God. Let me show you some scriptures that express this truth so clearly. In Psalm 19:1, we are told,

> *The heavens declare the glory of God; and the firmament shows His handiwork.*

Creation is the first miracle recorded in the Bible. We are told that it declares God's glory.

There is a scripture that I have loved since I was a teenager. It is in 2 Corinthians 1:20:

> *For all the promises of God in Him are Yes, and in Him Amen, to the glory of God through us.*

What a beautiful promise we are given here! Supposedly, there are 7,487 promises in the Bible, which belong to us through the sacrifice and the finished work of the cross. I love it when I see God fulfill His promises in the lives of His children through a miracle. We must never forget that, when we see this happen, it is not only because God loves us, but also so that He might glorify His name.

Paul said that *"all the promises of God in Him are Yes, and in Him Amen, to the glory of God through us"* (2 Cor. 1:20). Since every fulfilled promise in our lives glorifies God, and God has a deep desire to glorify His own name, we can live in full assurance of faith that miracles, in order to fulfill any promise of God, are certainly what He desires to do.

Miracles must never be an end in themselves. Scripture tells us in 1 Corinthians 10:31, *"Therefore, whether you eat or drink, or whatever you do, do all to the glory of God."* Every miracle that we pursue and desire must be to the glory of God. If you truly want to glorify God with your life, you cannot live your life without manifestations of the supernatural. In my understanding, it is a contradiction to say that we want to glorify God in all we do but not experience the supernatural on a regular basis. We are told in Numbers 14:21, *"But truly, as I live, all the earth shall be filled with the glory of the LORD."*

The whole earth shall be filled with the glory of the Lord. What a beautiful promise. Since every miracle glorifies God, our hearts should desperately cry out for the supernatural manifestation of His great name in our daily lives. We are told in Romans 11:36, *"For of Him and through Him and to Him are all things, to whom be glory forever. Amen."* Forever God's name must be glorified, which will happen, among other things, through miracles.

To Destroy the Works of the Devil

Jesus was manifest in order to destroy the works of Satan, as we are told in 1 John 3:8, *"For this purpose the Son of God was manifested, that He might destroy the works of the devil."*

All around us people are bound because of the works of Satan. Jesus came to destroy those works. Sin, sickness, poverty, and destruction—all of these are works of Satan which Jesus came to destroy. Every time somebody who is sick receives a miraculous healing, the work of Satan has been exposed and destroyed once again.

As Christians, we have full authority over the devil, his demons, and all his dirty works in our lives. We must constantly remind ourselves that when the supernatural power of God exposes and destroys the work of Satan in anybody's life, it fulfills one of the purposes of the coming of Christ. Too easily we accept things the devil throws against us and respond in the natural, instead of responding in the supernatural. We should *expect* supernatural protection, provision, healing, and deliverance in our lives.

At times, Christians do not use their full authority over the devil because of their wrong understanding of the devil's authority or power. They believe he is God's opposite and, therefore, has a lot of power over their lives. The devil is not God's opposite, however, because God has no opposite. He is the creator of all things, and the devil is only one of his created beings.

My wife and I were celebrating one of our wedding anniversaries and drove home after a three-day vacation at the beach. It was late at night, and we were tired and looking for a suitable hotel to spend the night. When we finally found one, we went into our room and felt sick to our stomachs as soon as we stepped over the threshold. We wondered if it was from the dinner we had just eaten at a restaurant beforehand. But we were so tired that we immediately went to bed.

The hotel room was hot and stuffy; there was no window in the room and no air flow. We only covered ourselves with a sheet and tried to go to sleep. As we were lying on the bed, the sheet suddenly lifted itself off of our bodies. I immediately realized that there were demons in the room that wanted to cause us difficulties. In a quiet whisper, so as not to awaken my wife, whom I thought was already asleep, I said, "Devil, this is my room, not yours. I paid for it. Get out of here now."

Immediately, the sheet fell back on our bodies, and I did not feel sick to my stomach any longer. I asked my wife quietly if she was still awake, and she confirmed that she was. She told me that her nausea had also left her immediately. We are called to live in the miraculous in order to destroy the works of Satan.

Jesus constantly moved in the supernatural, bringing healings and miracles everywhere He went—and in doing so, He destroyed the works of the devil. Peter says in Acts 10:38,

> *How God anointed Jesus of Nazareth with the Holy Spirit and with power, who went about doing good and healing all who were oppressed by the devil, for God was with Him.*

When Jesus brought the supernatural power of God to earth, it expressed God's love, glorified His name, and also destroyed the works of Satan. There are other reasons why God loves to do miracles, but these three reasons should be enough for us to desperately desire them and radically believe that they can and must be part of every Christian's life.

Testimony

My name is Cintia, and I am 36. All through my adolescence, I had problems with my feet. I had a cast on them eight times. I used to have loose ligaments, and because of that, I was always afraid of stepping the wrong way on the floor and twisting my foot. I had physiotherapy sessions for many years, and I couldn't practice sports because I was afraid of getting hurt. When I was 32, I was walking, and my foot twisted again. I had to get a cast again, and I got really sad because I thought it would all start again. At that time, a person told me that there would be a conference in our church. I went to that meeting in a lot of pain, limping. When we were asked if there was a person feeling pain in the foot, I stood up and went to the front to receive some prayer. Then, I was asked to jump and run, which I immediately did. I left that place totally healed with strong feet. Today, I run four miles every day for the glory of God.

Testimony

My name is Israel, and I live in Goiânia, Brazil. When I was at the Bible school, I had a powerful class about the operations of the Holy Spirit. At the end of the class, we learned about the gifts, faith, healings, and miracles. We had a powerful moment in which we prayed, received prayer, and prophesied. Before the class finished, I received prayer because of my knee. I had had a surgery on my knee 14 days before that class, and I still had some stitches. The following week I went to the doctor. He asked me to kneel down and bend my knees, and I could do it. The doctor asked me to stop physiotherapy sessions because my knee was healed and there was no need to keep going. God did a miracle on my knee. I can do everything as if I had never had surgery.

Chapter 3

Truth or Facts

If we want to experience the supernatural on a constant basis, then we need to make the shift from believing the *facts* to believing the *truth*. There is a big difference between facts and truth. If we don't understand this, the supernatural will remain far from us. We must not think that we can use the supernatural in order to fulfill our dreams and desires. People have often suffered great disappointments because they thought that they could use faith to fulfil their own desires and dreams. Jesus told us that if we abide in Him and *His words* abide in us, we will receive anything we desire. It is not our dreams; it is His Word that will be fulfilled by faith. The promises of the Word of God are the only basis for the supernatural.

It Is Never Too Late for a Miracle

When I was 16 years old, I injured my back in an accident and lived with three herniated discs for many years. I went through weeks of very strong pain even to the point of feeling numbness in my right leg. Sometimes the pain was more intolerable than at other times. I was in constant pain for many years.

One day, many years into my ministry, I had to travel to another country to preach and was believing God for my back miracle. It was hard for me to imagine traveling and preaching in the condition I was in. As the time neared for my departure and nothing had changed in my back, I started battling with thoughts and feelings of hoplessness.

The next night I woke up; when I looked at the clock, it was exactly 3:16 a.m., and I was wide awake with a strong sense of the presence of God in my room. I probably spent over an hour enjoying the sweet presence of the Lord before I fell back to sleep. The next night I woke up again with a strong sense of the presence of the Lord in my bedroom. As I looked at the clock, again it was 3:16 a.m. This repeated itself for about two weeks at exactly 3:16 every night. I was starting to look forward to the Lord's manifest presence in my bedroom every night at the same time. I knew it was God because it was at the same time to the minute every night.

After the two weeks, I woke up again at night with the same strong sense of the presence of God in my room, but this time it was 3:19 a.m. Instead of being excited, the first words that came out of my mouth were "Lord, You are late." Immediately, Jesus replied, "I am never late, and it is never too late for a miracle." I knew then that He would supernaturally heal my back, and it would not be too late. I don't remember the exact time frame for my healing, but one night, I went to bed meditating on the truth that I am *in Christ* and woke up completely healed.

The Difference between Facts and Truth

If we need to make a shift from believing the facts to believing the truth, then we, of course, need to know the difference between the two. Naturally, people tend to believe the facts over the truth because that is how we have been raised. The facts have to do with this natural environment, while the truth has to do with the spiritual world.

The facts are what we see with our natural eyes and feel with our natural senses. The truth can only be seen with the eyes of faith. It is a fact that humans cannot walk on top of water. Because of the law of physics, if you attempt to do this, you will sink, and it could cost you your life. However, the truth is that Jesus, as well as Peter, walked on water.

Jesus is the truth; therefore, everything He says is also the truth. He told us this in John 14:6: "Jesus said to him, 'I am the way, the truth, and the life. No one comes to the Father except through Me.'" It is very important for us to understand that Jesus is not *just* our Savior and the Son of God who *speaks* the truth. He *is* the truth. Therefore, everything that comes out of His mouth is the absolute truth, even if it opposes or defies the facts.

Today everything is relative. We are taught that truth is not absolute but relative; therefore, it is hard for people to experience the supernatural. Many times in our lives there will be a clash between facts and truth. We have to decide which we will believe if we want to experience the supernatural. When Jesus walked on the water, the eleven disciples were inside the boat which was carried by the water. When Peter saw Jesus, he asked Him if he could come, and Jesus told him to come.

Because the words came out of the mouth of Jesus, who is the truth, they had the spiritual power to defy the facts. Truth always overcomes the facts, if we choose to believe it and obey it. Many times, when I was preaching at different places, God gave me words of knowledge about people with various sicknesses and diseases. He told me that He would heal those people at that moment. I boldly declared the truth in the face of the facts and said to the people, "Jesus will heal you now." Often my translators translated by saying, "Jesus *wants* to heal you now." I always corrected them and said, "No, He not only *wants* to; He *will*."

This happened again very recently when I prayed for a man who could not raise his arm because of an injury in his shoulder. The Lord told me He would heal him, but nothing happened when I prayed. I had to make a choice: Do I believe the fact, which was what I saw with my natural eyes and what the doctors said, or do I believe the truth? I chose to believe the truth and refused to give in one moment. I kept commanding the arm to lift up until the truth finally defied the fact. The man was completely healed.

Countless times in my life I have had to choose what I believe—facts or truth. When the Word of God and your circumstances disagree, you have to make a choice: will you believe the truth or the facts? God's Word is always the absolute truth, without debate. This is where the battle is often lost, and we miss a miracle. The facts scream loudly at us through our feelings or what we see with our natural eyes, while the truth sometimes only whispers in our hearts. We see this beautifully illustrated in Matthew 14:22–29:

> *Immediately Jesus made His disciples get into the boat and go before Him to the other side, while He sent the multitudes away. And when He had sent the multitudes away, He went up on the mountain by Himself to pray. Now when evening came, He was alone there. But the boat was now in the middle of the sea, tossed by the waves, for the wind was contrary. Now in the fourth watch of the night Jesus went to them, walking on the sea. And when the disciples saw Him walking on the sea, they were troubled, saying, "It is a ghost!" And they cried out for fear. But immediately Jesus spoke to them, saying, "Be of good cheer! It is I; do not be afraid." And Peter*

answered Him and said, "Lord, if it is You, command me to come to You on the water." So He said, "Come." And when Peter had come down out of the boat, he walked on the water to go to Jesus.

In this story, we clearly see how the truth always wins over the facts, if we believe and obey. The moment that Jesus said to Peter that he should come and walk on the water, His Word was the absolute truth. The truth of the Word of God even defied the law of physics. Everything you see with your natural eyes, even if it has been scientifically proven, is nothing but fact. God's Word is nothing but the truth.

If we can grasp this simple revelation and make a radical choice to believe the truth over the fact every time they oppose each other, we will live in the supernatural. Eleven disciples chose to believe the facts over the truth, stayed in the boat, and, therefore, never experienced the supernatural. People who walk in the supernatural never believe the facts over the truth.

Believing the truth over the facts is often very risky. The eleven disciples stayed in their boat of security while Peter took the risk and left the boat. One of the main reasons why people are afraid to believe the truth when it opposes the facts is because they find security in the facts as opposed to the truth. If you truly believe the truth, you have to risk, which sometimes causes people to be afraid.

If God tells you to leave everything and go to another country as a missionary, without any material support, then you have to risk. If God tells you not to listen to what the doctors told you but to firmly stand on His Word, which promises that you are healed, then you have to risk. If God tells you, as He did to me recently, to take a man who lost his ability to walk because of an accident, grab him by the hand, and pull him up, telling him to walk in the name of Jesus, then you have to risk. I have experienced countless miracles in my ministry. Most of them I experienced when I was willing to risk and believe the truth over the facts.

The eleven disciples chose to believe the facts over the truth, preferring their natural security over the risk of believing the truth and walking on water; therefore, they did not experience the supernatural in that situation. We need to raise the question here: which is better, to stay in a seemingly secure boat without Jesus, or to walk on the stormy sea with Jesus? Believing the facts and staying in the boat was, in reality, not secure because of the negative circumstances which they were facing. The story tells us that the wind and the waves were against the boat. What seemed to be secure was, in reality, not secure. It was safer to walk on water *with* Jesus than to stay in the boat without Him. I don't believe that we should ever ignore the facts or deny them. We should look them in the eye and then boldly declare the truth.

My Own Experience

Years ago, I was asked to teach at a seminary for one week and then preach at a conference at that same church on the weekend after the seminary. Just a couple of days before my trip, I had an accident where I fell and smashed my shoulder. I was in excruciating pain, which kept me awake all night in spite of strong painkillers. In the morning, I went to the doctor who sent me to the hospital, where they took an MRI to clearly see what was wrong. They then sent me to a specialist. The specialist said that he had to perform surgery immediately or else my shoulder would probably remain stiff and immovable.

I contacted the pastor who asked me to teach at the seminary and told him that I had to cancel due to the accident. He agreed with me about cancelling the seminary but asked me to still come and preach at the conference. My first thought was that I could not do that because I had to have surgery immediately and then would need time to recuperate. At that moment, the Lord spoke to my heart and told me, "Go and preach at the conference."

The doctor strongly advised me against it—being sure of the consequences which I would surely suffer. The facts were screaming into my ear, the excruciating pain speaking with a very loud voice, but I made a choice to believe the truth.

One of my friends told me that I must not be so stupid. She said that she would tell Debi, my wife, to stop me from going. I had already talked to Debi who told me that if God told me to go I had to go. I decided to believe the truth over the facts and arrived at the conference in a lot of pain.

In the middle of my very first message, the Lord spoke to my heart and said, "Stop preaching and call the sick to come to the front." I asked the first person who responded what her problem was, and she said that she had an injured shoulder. God healed her instantly. The next four people all had shoulder injuries, and all were instantly healed. What would have happened if I had stayed in my boat of security and believed the facts over the truth?

When I returned home from the conference, my shoulder was still in a lot of pain, but it was not stiff. I began a very painful therapy through which my shoulder was completely restored without surgery in just a few weeks. When I went back to the specialist, he told me that in more than 30 years of practice as a shoulder surgeon he had never seen anything like that.

The Heart of Unbelief

The Bible warns us in Hebrews 3:12 about a heart of unbelief: *"Beware, brethren, lest there be in any of you an evil heart of unbelief in departing from the living God."* These are very strong words, calling a heart of unbelief evil or perverse. The reason why a heart of unbelief is so evil in the eyes of God is because it believes the facts over the truth.

Since we have come to understand that the Word of God is always the truth, any promise in the Bible is then the truth, even if it is completely contrary to our circumstances. A Canadian professor counted the promises of God made to us in the Bible. He counted 7,487 promises. Each one of them is the truth which will often oppose the facts in our lives. What will you choose to believe—the truth or the facts?

Since I was a teenager, I have loved 2 Corinthians 1:20: *"For all the promises of God in Him are Yes, and in Him Amen, to the glory of God through us."* Here we have the guarantee that the 7,487 truths in the Bible are 100 percent reliable, even though they may stand against 7,487 facts. Scripture tells us that *all* of the promises of God are yes in Him, which is Jesus Christ.

They are not the truth because we believe them; they are the truth because Jesus Christ paid for them on the cross. When Jesus shouted, "It is finished!" He signed 7,487 blank checks with His blood. Your part is to believe them against any facts. By doing so, you will experience the supernatural power of God.

This scripture ends with this statement: "To the glory of God through us." Every time you believe the truth over the facts, God gets glorified.

The important part are the last two words which say, "through us." Christ has already done everything which needs to be done. Only through *believing* the truth will we experience the supernatural.

Testimony

My name is Junior. My son and I took part in a conference, but we arrived there during the time of the prayer. I had a lot of pain in my ear. I was invited to go to the front, and I received prayer. I was immediately healed. It was powerful. It edified me a lot because it was the first time I experienced the supernatural. Glory to the name of Jesus!

Chapter 4

Greek Philosophical Thinking

We do not have time for an in-depth study of this important subject, but since church history proves that Greek thinking is a huge hindrance to the supernatural, we have to address it here. One of the reasons why the early church moved in such power and authority was because Greek thinking was not part of their mindset. It infiltrated the church around the second century. Unfortunately, even now, the church is still deeply influenced by it. We must renounce and radically remove this thinking from our lives. It must be rooted out ruthlessly if we want the supernatural to become our lifestyle.

How Were We Raised?

Since we were not raised in the Hebrew culture, we were influenced by Greek thinking, which is contrary to the Hebrew mind or biblical thinking. I used to read my Bible not understanding the thinking patterns of the writers, who were Hebrews, living in a biblical culture. When I was in my early twenties, I learned that the western civilization that I grew up in resembled Greek or Hellenistic thinking and that the differences between Greek and Hebrew mindsets touch every area of our lives.

If I took a water bottle and asked a group of people to describe it to me, most people would say something like this: "It is about 15 centimeters tall; it is clear with a blue cap, etc." They are describing the way the bottle looks; which is typical of Greek thinking. Greek thinking is interested in form. However, those with a Hebrew perspective would describe the same bottle very differently. Their perspective would be more likely to describe the function or purpose. They would tell me that it is a container for holding water.

Hebrew thinking is God-centered and always monotheistic. We are told in Deuteronomy 6:4, *"Hear, O Israel: the LORD our God, the LORD is one!"* In the Hebrew mindset, God is at the center of everything in life. The Greeks, on the other hand, served a pantheon of gods and saw man as the center of life. We can see this everywhere in our modern societies. Humanism is a philosophy that takes this idea to a higher plane, eliminating the need for God or religion. Many of our churches have been infiltrated by this thinking, as we can witness through many modern worship songs. How many songs do we sing that are more about what God does for us (man-centered) than who He is (God-centered)?

Some Important Differences between Greek and Hebrew Thinking

Greeks were interested in outward things like beauty, the pursuit of pleasure, sexuality, and exposing parts of their bodies. We can see this everywhere in our modern society today. In contrast, the Hebrew way of thinking placed no more emphasis on the outer man than on the inner man. Spirituality, which expressed itself in a lively relationship with God and community, was the heart of Jewish worship. The human body was appreciated and cared for as a gift from the Lord. It was treated with respect and modesty as the vehicle through which the worship of God was performed. As we look around ourselves with this in view and see how much emphasis is placed on the outward, physical appearance, we can see that Greek thinking dominates our minds.

Education for the sake of gaining knowledge is also a Greek concept. Hebrew thinking highly values education as a tool to enable us to serve God and community more effectively. Let me show you the main differences in Greek and Hebrew education: the Greeks prepare, train, and educate individuals to serve the country, while Hebrews prepare individuals to serve God. Greeks teach students to trust their country and their government, while the Hebrews teach their students to trust God in all things. The Greeks prepare their students for their country, while the Hebrews prepare their students for eternity. Greeks focus on self-esteem and emotional adjustment, while the Hebrews discover God-given gifts and talents and develop them to their fullest potential.

You may wonder what all of this has to do with a book about the supernatural, which is a fair question. Many years ago, when I studied about the supernatural, I found out that the more Greek thinking there is in the minds of the people, the harder it is for them to believe and walk in the supernatural. In this chapter, I want to show you how much we have been influenced by this thinking so we can renounce it and turn from it.

What are the results of this difference in education? Greek thinkers are self-centered. Their attitude is "my will be done." Violence, corruption, and such things are a normal part of their society. Hebrew thinkers are God-centered. Their attitude is "Your will be done." They exercise authority with responsibility. They also have high morals and values. Look around you in society, and you will easily see what thinking influences us.

There is also a great difference in how Greek and Hebrew thinkers define success. To Greek thinkers, worldly success is defined by external values such as beauty, brauwn, higher education, money, and fame. They ask the question, "How will this benefit me?" However, Hebrew thinkers seek after success God's way. They put God first and understand that spiritual growth will impact every area of life. They are interested in living by God's rules, understanding that this is true success. They ask this question: "Have I done the will of my Father, and have I cleaved to my Beloved?" If we think about the heroes which modern society chooses, we will get further insight into how Greek thinking has influenced us. If your heroes, for instance, are models, actors, or sports figures, you are most likely looking at life with a Greek mindset. If, however, your heroes are people like Moses, David, Jesus, or even somebody who is impacting his community through godly lifestyle and action, you are most likely thinking with a Hebrew mindset.

How Greek and Hebrew thinkers approach philosophy is also very different. The Greek thinkers are lawless. Their attitude is "to each his own." They look out for number one. In their culture and mindset, there are no absolutes. To the Hebrew thinkers, however, there is lawfulness. They believe in loving one another and that the last shall be first. In their thinking, they need to deny themselves and obey God.

As Christians who desire to live a supernatural lifestyle, we must conform to God's way of thinking, which permeates the Bible. It is my conviction that we will not be able to live experientially in the supernatural on a constant basis unless we renounce all Greek thinking and embrace the Hebrew mindset.

Testimony

I live in Sanclerlândia, a small city in Goiás, Brazil. For some weeks, I had strong pain in both ears. My left ear was becoming clogged, and I could just hear in a dull way. There were nights that my husband had to wake up and pray with me, and sometimes I was sleeping with my hand over my ear because of the pain I felt. I participated in a conference, and the pastor started praying for the sick. The first person he called was someone who had problems in the ear, but I did not stand up. He kept calling, but I remained sitting. Then he told us about a person who was going through a similar situation; God wanted to heal that person, but they did not stand up to receive their healing. This testimony bothered me a lot. I never thought I would experience a miracle in my life. It seemed easier to see miracles in other people's lives. So, God started to move in me in such a way that I felt like a fire was burning into my heart. The pastor said God wanted to heal a person that had a problem in the ear, but did not know what it was. At that moment, I started crying, and then I stood up to receive prayer. I took a step of faith; I believed for my healing because I couldn't stand that pain anymore. I really wanted to be healed. I received some prayer, and I felt I was being healed. I never felt that pain again. I experienced the healing of the Lord in my life.

Chapter 5

The Kingdom of God

What Is the Kingdom of God?

There are many different views and opinions regarding the kingdom of God. Some believe that it is something that is only in the future. When Christ returns, He will set up His kingdom for 1000 years. Others believe that there will be no literal 1000-year kingdom of God. They believe that it is a spiritual kingdom which started with Jesus Christ and that the 1000 years simply means a long period of time. All the theologians who believe different things have valid biblical proof for what they believe.

I personally believe that the kingdom of God is both here and now and a literal 1000-year reign of Christ on earth. If we do not believe in the kingdom already being here and now, we will miss the supernatural power of God. We will constantly be waiting for something to be happening in the future, which God wants to take place now. We must see the power of God's kingdom in our everyday lives.

When Jesus lived on earth, He demonstrated the power of the kingdom. In Luke 11:20, He said, *"But if I cast out demons with the finger of God, surely the kingdom of God has come upon you."* Jesus constantly cast out demons every place He went; therefore, the kingdom of God was upon the people everywhere Jesus went. This is very simple to understand. Every kingdom has a king who exercises authority. People were under the kingdom of darkness and oppressed by demons. Jesus came casting out those demons and bringing the authority of King Jesus upon them. We see that everywhere Jesus went He brought His kingdom to people who were willing to receive it.

When Jesus sets up His 1000-year reign on earth, His authority will be absolute. That means that all subjects of His kingdom will be fully surrendered to Him. Today His kingdom is not absolute because everyone can choose if they want to be under the authority of His kingship or not. Everybody who will be part of the 1000-year reign with Christ will be completely surrendered to Him.

At this present time, each person can choose if he or she wants to surrender to Him.

The Gospel of the Kingdom

Jesus not only preached the gospel; the Bible says specifically that He preached the *gospel of the kingdom*. I personally have heard plenty of preachers who did not preach the gospel of the kingdom. The gospel of the kingdom is a gospel where King Jesus demonstrates and exercises His power, authority, and lordship. It is a gospel of the supernatural, with signs and wonders following. In Matthew 4:23–25, we read,

> *And Jesus went about all Galilee, teaching in their synagogues, preaching the gospel of the kingdom, and healing all kinds of sickness and all kinds of disease among the people. Then His fame went throughout all Syria; and they brought to Him all sick people who were afflicted with various diseases and torments, and those who were demon-possessed, epileptics, and paralytics; and He healed them. Great multitudes followed Him—from Galilee, and from Decapolis, Jerusalem, Judea, and beyond the Jordan.*

As we look at this scripture, we see a direct connection between preaching the gospel of the kingdom and the supernatural. In the same sentence we read that Jesus preached the gospel of the kingdom and healed all kinds of sicknesses and diseases. This is more important for us to understand than many people realize. The word *gospel* means good news, or too-good-to-be-true-news, which must touch every part of our lives—body, soul, and spirit. Any gospel which is without the supernatural power of God to heal our sick bodies, radically transform our sinful nature, provide for us supernaturally, fill us with an inexpressible sense of joy and peace, and give us an eternally secure salvation in heaven is not the gospel of the kingdom.

Unfortunately, a large part of the church focuses mainly on the spiritual part, which is our eternal salvation. Many also focus on the material part, the financial blessing. However, the gospel of the kingdom must be seen and demonstrated in a radically supernatural way. Healings, miracles, and supernatural experiences must become a normal part of the preaching of the gospel.

We must never underestimate the importance of miracles in the preaching of the gospel. This is so clearly demonstrated throughout the New Testament. Recently, I preached in a church in Brazil where an atheist woman attended the meeting. The power of God healed her body which caused her to give her life to Jesus, and she is now part of that church, as well as a cell group.

Jesus showed us the importance of miracles in the preaching of the gospel when He gave His disciples the Great Commission, which we can read of in Mark 16:15–18,

> *And He said to them, "Go into all the world and preach the gospel to every creature. He who believes and is baptized will be saved; but he who does not believe will be condemned.* ***And these signs will follow those who believe:*** *In My name they will cast out demons; they will speak with new tongues; they will take up serpents; and if they drink anything deadly, it will by no means hurt them; they will lay hands on the sick, and they will recover.* (Emphasis mine)

Jesus said that these supernatural signs would follow everybody who believes. I cannot understand how we have separated miracles from evangelism. These two must go hand-in-hand. Radical evangelism will never be without the demonstration of the power of God. When Jesus sent out His disciples, in Matthew 10:7–8, He not only told them to preach the gospel, but also to demonstrate His power among the people:

> *And as you go, preach, saying, "The kingdom of heaven is at hand." Heal the sick, cleanse the lepers, raise the dead, cast out demons. Freely you have received, freely give.*

Many more people would get saved if we would combine evangelism with the supernatural as a normal part of the preaching of the gospel. This truth is seen several times in Scripture. We see this in John 2:23: "Now when He was in Jerusalem at the Passover, during the feast, many believed in His name when they saw the signs which He did." The miracles were the reason why people believed. We must not limit the supernatural only to our meetings in church, but take it out on the streets combined with evangelism. That seemed to be the practice of the early church. As we can see in Acts 8:5–8,

Then Philip went down to the city of Samaria and preached Christ to them. And the multitudes with one accord heeded the things spoken by Philip, **hearing and seeing the miracles which he did.** *For unclean spirits, crying with a loud voice, came out of many who were possessed; and many who were paralyzed and lame were healed. And there was great joy in that city.* (Emphasis mine)

There was a powerful revival in the city of Samaria because there was radical evangelism. Philip not only preached the gospel, but he also demonstrated its power with many miracles. The Bible says that they listened and responded when they saw and heard the miracles which he did. Jesus said in John 14:11, *"Believe Me that I am in the Father and the Father in Me, or else believe Me for the sake of the works themselves."*

Not Words but Power

We are told in 1 Corinthians 4:20, *"For the kingdom of God is not in word but in power."* Since the Bible is the absolute truth, we must believe that the kingdom of God is not words, but the supernatural power of God. To put it in simple words, the gospel of the kingdom is too-good-to-be-true-news which is demonstrated in the supernatural power of a loving God for our benefit.

Most Christians know the Lord's Prayer, which I want you to read here out loud. Matthew 6:9–12 says,

> *In this manner, therefore, pray: Our Father in heaven, hallowed be Your name. Your kingdom come. Your will be done on earth as it is in heaven. Give us this day our daily bread. And forgive us our debts, as we forgive our debtors.*

Let us interpret the Bible by the Bible. Remember that Paul said that the kingdom of God is power. Jesus taught us to pray for His kingdom to come. I am putting the Lord's Prayer here again, but I am exchanging the word *kingdom* for *power*. Please read this prayer again out loud and emphasize the word *power*:

> *In this manner, therefore, pray: Our Father in heaven, hallowed be Your name. Your power come. Your will be done on earth as*

it is in heaven. Give us this day our daily bread. And forgive us our debts, as we forgive our debtors.

It was the Lord Jesus Himself who taught us this prayer; therefore, it must become the heart-cry of every Christian. When I understood this more than 30 years ago, I began to cry out to God constantly for His power to come. Unfortunately, Christians have developed a theology over the centuries, where miracles are the exception and not the norm.

I talked to a pastor from Poland yesterday who was told by other pastors in that nation that he needs to stop emphasizing and pursuing the supernatural and miracles in his ministry. As we discussed that, we realized that all the pastors who told him this are people who do not experience the supernatural power of the kingdom in their ministries.

Testimony

In 2014, I was diagnosed with three herniated discs. One day, I tried to get up, but I fell on the floor. I had very strong pain in my back, and my legs were paralyzed. I was taken to hospital. The doctors did an MRI and found out that I had three herniated discs at the end of my back that were pressuring the nerve and stopped me from walking. For three months, the doctors tried a treatment via medications and rest, but it brought no results. They changed the medications, but after two months, there was still no improvement. It was a critical situation, so they started thinking about surgery. Surgery could make my situation even worse because it could cause greater damage that would put me in a wheelchair forever. After some physiotherapy and acupuncture sessions, I started to recover movement little by little. But I still had some crises that paralyzed me for a few days. I was tired of the situation, the medications, and the treatments. The doctor suggested that I change my profession because of this problem. I felt like the bleeding woman from the Bible. I was outraged, and I knew that only a touch of God could change my situation.

I received two prophetic words during a *Seminary of Faith* that I participated in. One was about my profession, and the other was about my healing. As I received prayer, I felt very strong heat on my back as I had never felt before. I knew I was being healed. At the next appointment with the physiotherapist, my body responded to all stimuli and exercises. The physiotherapist asked me if I had prayed (I was preaching the gospel to her and always told her about the healing promise over my life), and I answered, "I am healed!" She examined me and could see I was really fine. I went back to work after the doctor authorized me. I could jump and praise the Lord with freedom once more and never felt the pain caused by the hernias again. During that difficult time, I was moved by the book, *Mountain-Moving Faith* by Reinhard Hirtler, and I decided to believe in God despite the negative diagnosis. I praise the Lord for everything I went through because I grew stronger and my faith was renewed. God is amazing!

Chapter 6

The Kingdom of God, Continued

Reaching Dark Places

Austria used to be called the graveyard of the missionaries. It was called that because most missionaries who went there died in their mission-pursuits, never seeing any converts. Many of them left the country disillusioned and depressed. It is the country where I was born and raised. Most churches there are very small, and there are hundreds of towns without a single Christian. The estimated number of evangelical believers, counting all denominations together is 0.5 percent. Many of my pastor friends worked for decades trying to plant churches with very little success. I personally know of pastors who did not see anybody saved under their ministry in 15 years.

Thirty years ago, when we planted our first church, we had no money, no building, and no support; we only had faith. We went into the first town, printed bright yellow posters with big black letters that said, "Healing for body, soul, and spirit.

Come and receive it for free." We also wrote on those posters that every night for the following two weeks people could experience this at the place we rented. Many esoteric and sick people who had never been to church in their lives showed up. I preached a 20-minute gospel message and prayed for everybody to experience the supernatural power of God. The sick got healed, the oppressed got delivered, and the kingdom of God was present.

I remember that one whole esoteric cell group got saved except for the husband of the leader of the cell group.[1] We burned esoteric books in our backyard worth way over $30,000. The leader of this esoteric cell group wanted me to visit her home and meet her husband. When I arrived, she had a lot of good Austrian chocolate, which I loved, on the table. They were all individually wrapped in aluminum foil.

Throughout the evening, while talking to her husband, I ended up eating the whole box. Her husband got up and got his divining rod. He focused the rod on the pile of aluminum foil next to me and told me that it radiated negative energy and that I should remove it. His divining rod elevated very high in his hands. I looked at him and said, "Nothing can harm me. I am in Jesus." His divining rod instantly dropped, and no matter how hard he tried, he could not get it to elevate again. In shock, he said that he had never seen anything like that.

Then he focused his divining rod on my head in order to measure my aura. The divining rod elevated so forcefully that it almost fell out of his hands. This was a man who was deeply involved in the esoteric and in witchcraft. When he told me that he had never seen such a powerful aura, I shared the gospel of the kingdom with him. He got saved and became a faithful member of our church.

The Example of Paul

Paul not only preached the gospel; he preached and demonstrated the gospel of the kingdom. In Acts 19:8–12, we read,

> *And he went into the synagogue and spoke boldly for three months, reasoning and persuading concerning the things of the kingdom of God. But when some were hardened and did not believe, but spoke evil of the Way before the multitude, he departed from them and withdrew the disciples, reasoning daily in the school of*

Tyrannus. And this continued for two years, so that all who dwelt in Asia heard the word of the Lord Jesus, both Jews and Greeks. Now God worked unusual miracles by the hands of Paul, so that even handkerchiefs or aprons were brought from his body to the sick, and the diseases left them and the evil spirits went out of them.

Paul preached the gospel of the kingdom in verse 8, and we see in verse 11 that God worked unusual miracles through him. If we preach the right gospel, we will always see the right results. We must reject a theology where the gospel is only about saving the lost. That is not the gospel of the kingdom.

The Promise of Jesus

Jesus made a promise regarding the end times. In Matthew 24:14, He told us, *"And this gospel of the kingdom will be preached in all the world as a witness to all the nations, and then the end will come."* Jesus did not just say that the *gospel* will be preached; He specifically said that the *gospel of the kingdom* will be preached. Remember what the kingdom is? It is not words, but power. How have we developed a theology where the preaching of the gospel is words only?

I carry a deep conviction in my heart that before the return of Christ there will be a church that walks in the true power of the kingdom. When Jesus told His disciples in Matthew 10:7–8 to *preach the gospel of the kingdom, He told them to heal the sick, cleanse the lepers, raise the dead, and cast out demons.* Let us preach the kingdom.

Let us look at another scripture most Christians know. Matthew 6:33 says, *"But seek first the kingdom of God and His righteousness, and all these things shall be added to you."*

I understand that the expression "the kingdom of God" has several different meanings and applications. Certainly, as we have seen in 1 Corinthians 4:20, one of the expressions of the kingdom of God is the manifestation of His glorious supernatural power which is an expression of His love.

Now let us look at Matthew 6:33 with this application. Jesus said that we should seek first the kingdom (power) of God. One of the meanings of the Greek word *zēteite* which is translated here for *seek* means to crave for and demand from someone.[1]

Let me tell you, my dear friend, Jesus told us to crave for and demand the power of God first and foremost. What an incredible revelation this is. Jesus said it in the context of our concerns for our material needs. How much energy, thought, prayer, and effort go into our material provision? This should not be so at all. Maybe you say, "But I need to provide for my family and for my needs." This is an earthly way of thinking, which should have no part in the life of a Christian.

We should strongly reject this mentality as Jesus tells us to do in Matthew 6. We should crave, first and foremost, His incredible supernatural power, which is an expression of His deep love for humanity, and demand from God that it will be manifest in and through our lives. If we do so with all of our hearts and wholeheartedly fulfill the second part of this scripture—to seek His righteousness alone (which is by faith in the finished work of the cross)—we will live in the supernatural provision of heaven, which is limitless.

If you find this difficult to believe, I encourage you to read my book *Prosperity*. It is interesting, that Jesus puts these two things together and says that we should seek God's kingdom and His righteousness. If we have an inclination to find righteousness in what we do and in our works for the Lord, even moving in the supernatural, we have not understood or obeyed this commandment of Jesus. Because we are perfectly righteous in Christ Jesus alone, we now have no option but to crave for and demand from God that His supernatural power flows from us to the lost world He loves so deeply.

One meaning of *righteousness* is "acceptance." We must crave for, seek, and receive by faith the acceptance of God because of the sacrifice of Jesus alone, not because we move in the supernatural and are channels of the power of God. If we seek one apart from the other, we will not be useful for God in the way He desires. If we only seek His righteousness (acceptance)—and not also His supernatural power flowing through us—we will become selfish and self-centered Christians who will not fulfill God's purpose in our lives. If, on the other hand, we seek the supernatural power of God flowing through us, and through it try to get righteousness (acceptance), we will become hard-hearted, proud, and possibly even hurtful and destructive people.

Another meaning of *kingdom* is "colonization." When a kingdom took over another country, they not only invaded that country, but the culture of the invading kingdom was forced upon the country being conquered and its people. The invaded country and its people had no option at all. They began to act, speak, and even, over time, to think like the people of the kingdom that invaded them.

You can still see this today in various places of the world. The Bahamas is a very hot place, yet in the afternoons, in ridiculously hot temperatures, people drink hot black tea with milk. Why would they do such a strange thing—and not drink nice, cool drinks? Because they were invaded by the British kingdom, and the British people drink their hot black tea with milk in the afternoons.

Since God is neither a tyrant nor a control freak, He gave us the free will to choose if we will surrender to His kingdom or not. This is one of the reasons why so few people see the supernatural power of God expressed through their lives. The kingdom of God does not invade us; it is near us, and we must crave for it and demand it from heaven.

I encourage you to carefully study the four Gospels and look at how Jesus brought the supernatural power of God everywhere He went because He was surrendered to the purpose of the kingdom of His Father. You and I must do the same thing. The kingdom of God is near you; please crave for it and demand it from God, and it will invade your life.

Endnotes

1. *Esoteric* individuals are those who seek spiritual things and are very open and hungry for mystical things, but seek them in the occult, believing that it is God. For instance, they will not pray directly to God and ask for direction; instead, they will ask the divining rod, use tarot cards, and table levitation, etc.

2. Zéteó, "to seek," Strong's #2212; http://biblehub.com/greek/2212.htm, accessed 15 September 2016.

Testimony

My name is Erica, and I am part of Videira Itaquera, Brazil. I want to tell you what God did in my son's life through *Seminary of Faith*. My baby was four months old, and he suffered from a clogged intestine.

Sometimes, he didn't have a stool for seven days. The pastor called some people to receive prayer and be healed, especially those who had problems in the intestines. I stood up and, by faith, I took my son's healing. At that specific moment, my baby hadn't excreted for four days, and he had strong cramps. That same day, after prayer, he could excrete, and his intestines started working regularly every day. He never suffered with cramps again. My son was healed for the honor and the glory of the Lord Jesus. Hallelujah

Chapter 7

The Supernatural in Church History

I will now ask three important questions: 1) Have there always been miracles throughout the history of the church in the dimension that they happened through Christ and His apostles? 2) Why have some people experienced more miracles than others? 3) What can we learn from history?

Let us answer the first question and look at church history.

From the End of the First Century to the Fifth Century

Justin Martyr (100–165) wrote a letter to the Roman Senate in which he said that many Christians in his churches and towns were casting out demons, healing the sick, and exercising great authority.

Irenaeus, Bishop of Lyons (130–202) spoke extensively of miracles which Christians performed. He talked about the gifts of the Spirit and their outstanding results through "ordinary" Christians. He wrote of the many Christians who prophesied things of the future and had visions; others healed the sick through the laying on of hands. He even spoke of resurrections of the dead. Many of the miracles he experienced firsthand; others he heard from reliable witnesses. He constantly emphasized that the miracles were not just for some special people, but for the whole body of Christ.

Perpetua and *Felicitas* were two women who died as martyrs in the year 202 or 203. They were powerfully used in prophetic revelations and visions. Many of the visions, which were very specific, have been recorded in a German booklet called *Die Leidenschaft der Heiligen Maertyrer Perpetua and Felicitas*; the English title is *The Passion of Perpetua and Felicity*.

Tertullian (c. 155–225) was known as the greatest theologian of his time. He wrote about the charismatic gifts. He experienced the supernatural as a normal part of Christian life. When he baptized people, he taught them that when they came out of the water, they should pray and expect to receive the gifts of the Spirit.

Eusebius (c. 260–340) was known as the father of church history. He was delighted about manifold use of the gifts of the Spirit among

Christians. Many stories of miracles, healings, words of knowledge, words of wisdom, and supernatural faith through Christians have been recorded by him.

Athanasius (c. 296–373), the famous bishop of the African town Alexandria, was a courageous opponent of heresies. He wrote in a letter that he personally knew Christians who performed extraordinary miracles.

Bishop Hilary of Poitiers (c. 315–c. 367) said that in his church the gifts of the Spirit, such as miracles, healings, prophecies, and the like, were regularly exercised.

Martin Bishop of Tours (died 397) exercised miracles in the dimension of the apostles. He destroyed heathen altars and preached the gospel with incredible signs following. He cast out devils, healed the sick, and even raised the dead.

Bishop Epiphanius of Salamis (c. 315–403): miracles were part of his daily life. He constantly prophesied and had very accurate words of knowledge.

Cyril of Jerusalem (315–385) told people when they got saved that they should not only expect forgiveness of their sins but also miracles in the same dimension that the apostles performed them. He told people that if they believed, not only would their sins be forgiven, but they would also perform miracles which supercede every human power. He told people to prepare themselves to receive the heavenly gifts.

Augustine (354—430) wrote a diary in the fifth century about the miracles which he experienced. He talked about the resurrection of a young man, as well as many healings of cripples, cancers, fractured bones, blind eyes, and deliverance from demons. He also talked about people who fell to the ground by the power of God and got back up healed. He said that those miracles were by no means only happening through the bishops.

The Sayings of the Desert Fathers is a collection of miracles that happened in the fourth and fifth centuries.[1] They tell about a whole number of "ordinary" Christians through whom miracles happened on a regular basis. Words of knowledge, healings, deliverance from demons, and other miracles were part of the daily lives of these "ordinary" Christians. One story tells about Joseph of Panephysis who was visited by a Christian who came from a long distance to ask him about fasting. Before she could ask the question, Joseph gave her the answer, over which this Christian was astonished and glorified God.

The Middle Ages

In the early Middle Ages, many stories of signs, wonders, and miracles continue.

Severus of Antioch (465–538) wrote down many accounts of signs, wonders, and miracles done through "ordinary" Christians.

Benedict of Nursia (480–550) shook Italy through his powerful healings, miracles, and prophecies.

Gregory Bishop of Tours (c. 540–594) wrote chronicles about miracles. He wrote about countless miracles which were performed by Christians all over Europe. He wrote in order to prove that miracles did not cease with the apostles, but were still normal in his time.

In the seventh century, there was an explosion of miracles all over Great Britian.

Aidan Bishop of Linisfarne (died 651), together with his successor *Cuthbert (c. 634–687),* performed outstanding miracles. It has been told that the blind saw, cripples walked, and even the dead were raised. When Cuthbert was a child, he received a prophecy from a three-year-old friend that one day he would be a priest. He performed such powerful miracles that everywhere he went people in need surrounded him. He prophesied very accurately what would happen in their lives; these prophecies were then fulfilled.

From the eighth to the eleventh centuries, there are reports of signs and wonders from all over the world.

Joseph Hazzaya (born c. 710) of Syria reported how, through him and many other Christians, signs and wonders were performed. He wrote about exuberant praise and speaking in other tongues.

Ulrich of Augsburg (c. 890–973) performed miracles all over Germany.

Anselm of Canterbury (c. 1033–1109) performed signs, wonders, and miracles all over England. He also moved very strongly in the prophetic.

William of Malmesbury (c. 1095–1143) and *Orderic Vitalis (c. 1075–1142)* collected reports of miracles and healings in their time. They wrote of many healings and miracles as well as words of knowledge. People like *Hugh of Lincoln (c. 1140–1200)* in England and *Bernard of Clairveaux (1090–1153)* in France particularly stick out for powerfully moving in the supernatural in those reports.

Francis of Asissi (1182–1226) performed many signs and wonders.

Thomas Aquinas (1225–1274) was, without doubt, the greatest theologian of the Middle Ages. In *Summa Theologica*, he wrote that God did powerful miracles through "ordinary" Christians. He wrote about the importance of the gift of prophecy.

Catherine of Siena (1347–1380) was probably the person who performed the greatest miracles in the fourteenth century. She was one of only two women in church history who received the title Doctor of the Church. She raised the dead, had very precise and outstanding words of knowledge for individual people, and even kings asked for her counsel. It is said that one day she wrote a letter to the pope in which she rebuked him for making an oath to the Lord that he did not keep. The pope never talked to anyone about that oath. She had a word of knowledge.

From the End of the Middle Ages to Today

George Fox (1624–1691) was the founder of the Quakers. He kept a diary in which he wrote down the miracles that he experienced. It is filled with stories of supernatural healings.

John Wesley (1703–1791), founder of the Methodists, wrote in his diary countless stories of miracles and supernatural healings. These miracles either happened through him or were personally witnessed by him as they took place through other people.

Nicolaus of Zinzendorf (1700–1760) wrote that apostolic powers were active in his churches. He

83

talked about signs, wonders, and incurable diseases like cancer being healed. He also wrote about people who were already in the last stages of death being instantly healed, sometimes when a single word was spoken to them.

Johann Blumhardt (1805–1880), the German pastor, experienced outstanding miracles in his life. In 1843, he prayed for a girl who was dying, and she was supernaturally healed. His miracles became a sensation in Europe.

Dorothea Trudel (1813–1862) made headlines in 1851. The young Swiss florist anointed some of her workmates who were so sick that no medical treatment helped them. When she anointed them with oil, they were instantly healed. People from the entire continent of Europe came to her and experienced many miracles.

Charles Cullis (1833–1892) was a doctor in Boston, MA. In 1870, he witnessed a woman who had been paralyzed for five months because of a brain tumor get immediately, supernaturally healed through prayer. That changed his life. He spent the rest of his life praying for the sick and making miracles a reality amongst all Christians. His influence upon other men of God was so great that many of them opened themselves up for the supernatural and their churches began to experience miracles. Some of those men of God were Andrew Murray, founder of a Christian Missionary Society; A.B.Simpson; and A.J. Gordon.

William Branham (1909–1965) was one of the greatest healing evangelists of his century. There was no sickness which was able to stand before him. His words of knowledge were amazingly precise. In 1951, William Upshaw, a member of the California Congress who was paralyzed from birth, was suddenly healed by the prayer of William Branham. That became worldwide news.

Endnote

1. *The Sayings of the Desert Fathers;* see http://www.stmarkchicago.org/Selections-From-The-Sayings-Of-The-Desert-Fathers.pdfm, accessed 15 September 2016.

Testimony

My name is Simone, and I am a student at Videira Bible School in Boston, USA. My little toe was broken, and I went to the doctor. I had a lot of pain and couldn't step on the floor. Soon afterward, I participated at a conference in which God was moving. The pastor was praying, and he asked if there was a person who had any pain or disease. At that moment another pastor felt like praying for me. I really believed with all my heart when I received that prayer. After that, I could move my foot and do all the movements I couldn't do before; my little toe did not hurt anymore. I was healed at that very moment. I was impressed. I moved my toe, stepped on the floor, and there was no pain. The miracle really happened!

Testimony

My name is Israel. In a conference in Ribeirão Preto, Brazil, there was a great miracle in my son's life. Calebe had a disease called "hand-foot-and-mouth." He couldn't eat or drink water because he had sores that hurt a lot. He had fever and a lot of pain in his body. At the conference, there was a call for healing, and, immediately, my wife and I went to receive it. The pastor prayed for us. After that, we took our son to hospital. While we were waiting for the doctor, my son saw a child eating some chips, and he asked for some. I thought it wouldn't work, but Calebe started crying because he really wanted some. So we gave him some chips. He ate them without difficulty—and then we gave him some water, and he drank it as if he had no problems. My son was immediately healed, and the name of the Lord was glorified. Hallelujah! Hallelujah!

Chapter 8

The Supernatural in Church History, Continued

The Reliability of These Accounts

These accounts of miracles in church history are not just fantasy stories. They are very reliable. They were written down by eyewitnesses or people who personally performed them. Many of the people involved are recognized church fathers. Severus of Antioch is said to have observed, "I have not written down anything of which I had not accurate proofs. I would rather not write down anything and to remain silent than to write down things which are not true." At the beginning of the tenth century, all records of miracles were carefully investigated by the church fathers. No documentation of miracles was looked at unless they had the name of the person, their address, the exact sickness, the names of the witnesses, when and how the people encountered those who performed the miracle, and how the healing miracle manifested.

The Separation within the Church

Now we will answer the second question. Why have some people experienced more miracles than others? Around the beginning of the second century, there were *two terrible separations within* the church.

The first separation was that the church became institutional. Suddenly, laity and clergy became separate, which was not the case before then. The apostles did not consider themselves "professionals" in the ministry, but men who were called by God to equip every member for the ministry. People who were powerfully used by God throughout the centuries, as we have seen in this chapter, were people who refused to bow to this separation.

Before this separation, there were many bishops (presbytery) leading one church; after the separation, there was one bishop leading many churches. Before this separation, every member was a minister; after the separation, the ministry became professional. Before this separation there was no hierarchy or position; there were simply functions. After the separation, church government became a hierarchy. Before this separation, women were allowed to serve God; after the separation, women were forbidden to minister. Before this separation, everybody wore normal clothes; after the separation, the ministers began to wear special clothes which separated them from the laity.

At this point, I want you to carefully look into your own heart and mind. What do you believe regarding these five separations? Do you believe that full-time ministry is something special? Do you believe in a hierarchy—in which the pastor is more important than any other member of the church? Do you believe that pastors have to wear special, fancy clothes—different from any other member of the church? Do you believe that women cannot move in an equal anointing and demonstration of the supernatural as men can? If you answered yes to even one of these questions, your thinking is still influenced by what happened in the second century. It will greatly hinder you in experiencing the supernatural.

The second separation was that the church became intellectual. Augustine and Aquinas brought *Greek, philosophical* thinking into the church.

I will not talk much about this as I have dealt with it in a previous chapter. Just to give you a quick history, Augustine struggled with promiscuity which he was unable to overcome and which left him very disturbed.

He therefore accepted *Greek philosophical* thinking which separates, among other things, body and spirit. It teaches that God worked in the spirit of man and that the body was not important. Therefore, the sin in a person's body was not a big deal.

The worship of saints originates from this thinking because it separates the spiritual from the natural. The dead live in the spiritual world while people who are alive live in the natural world (in *their* thinking, of course). Therefore, it is better to pray to and worship a dead saint who is now alive in the spiritual world than to ask a living person who lives in the natural world and has no access to the spiritual world. Many biblical statements have been influenced by this thinking and have become spiritualized instead of being accepted in the sense in which they were written.

This has greatly limited the experience of the supernatural in the church. Jesus Himself said that anybody who believes in Him will do the same works that He did and greater ones. The reason why this is not experienced in the church at large is because we have accepted the Greek way of thinking.

For instance, *ideal* is not a Hebrew word; it is a Greek word. It is not *ideal* to have a sexual relationship between a husband and a wife only. Today, even some Christians think that this is the *ideal* way to have a relationship. It is not *ideal*; it is the *only* biblically correct way. Anything else is sin.

Toward the end of his life, Augustine changed his thinking, yet *Greek philosophical* thinking remained in the church. Until this very day, the majority of evangelical churches are more influenced by this thinking than by Hebrew thinking, which is what the apostle Paul meant.

Dynamic or Determined

Calvin spoke a lot against miracles in the body of Christ. He taught that God does miracles *however He wants and whenever He decides to do them* and that we have absolutely no influence over any miracle that will take place. He believed that our relationship with God is *determined*.

Arminius withstood Calvin. Arminius taught that our relationship with God is not *determined* but *dynamic*, meaning that God desires to do miracles and express His supernatural power through us depending on our response and reaction toward Him. He said that how much of the supernatural we experience depends on how we respond to Him and whether we believe and obey the truths of the Word of God. He taught that we will experience miracles in direct relation to our obedience and faith in the Word of God.

To explain the two sides together, let us take the following Bible verse: "These signs shall follow those who believe, in My name they shall lay hands on the sick and the sick shall recover." If you lay hands on the sick *hoping* that God will heal them (when and how He sees fit), you may see a miracle *occasionally* because you believe your relationship with God is *determined* by Him. In other words, whenever He is *determined* (if He wants to), He will heal the sick. However, if you lay hands on the sick with an absolute conviction in your heart that the sick have no other option but to get healed, you will see the supernatural, which is *dynamic*.

We are charismatic enough not to deny or reject the words of Jesus to lay hands on the sick. Because we are not convinced that our relationship is *dynamic* and what we experience is *determined* by our radical response, faith, and obedience to these words of Jesus, we do lay hands on the sick and pray—but not with the absolute conviction that they will be healed. In our relationship with God, we have mixed *dynamic* and *determined* in the wrong way. God has already determined to heal the sick, which is clearly written in the Word of God.

Learning the Lesson

Now let us answer the third question: what can we learn from history? One of the important lessons from history is that God has always moved in extraordinary miracles through "ordinary" people. As long as people were willing to take the Word of God seriously, reject wrong thinking, and do whatever it takes to see the power of God, He used them.

Another important lesson from history is that we have to reject clericalism. The five ministries—which are apostles, prophets, evangelists, pastors, and teachers—are not here to do the job and move in the supernatural. They are here to equip every member of the body of Christ to be a channel of the power of the kingdom of God. There are many more lessons we can learn from history which you may discover for yourself by studying church history on your own.

Testimony

There was a meeting in Belo Horizonte, Brazil, and at the end of it, the pastor called people to the front to receive prayer. He said something about sick fingernails. At that moment, I remembered that, when I was four, I hurt my finger, and my nail was damaged at its root. The doctors said they couldn't do anything to help me. That was something that bothered me quite a lot even though it did not hurt. The pastor started praying, and, even though my mind kept telling me that praying for that problem was pointless and insane, I prayed. Apparently, nothing happened at that moment, but I believed. Some months later, a miracle happened: The hole that I had had for decades in the middle of my nail just disappeared, and my nail became perfect. Thank You, Jesus!

Chapter 9

Signs and Wonders

Signs and wonders are supposed to be a normal part of the life of every believer. This was considered normal in the life of the early church.

What Are Signs?

The Hebrew word for *signs* is *owth* and means "a signal or a proof."[1] This word occurs 76 times in the Old Testment. The Greek word for *signs* is *semeion* and means the following: "A supernatural act through which God lets the people who were sent by Him appear trustworthy, or through which the people prove that what they say and do is from God."[2] This word occurs 77 times in the New Testament. God has a much greater desire to demonstrate signs and wonders than we do. Since God longs for all people to be saved and wants to prove to them that He truly is alive and that we are sent by Him to share the Good News, He wants to confirm our message with signs and wonders. The entire Bible, as well as church history, proves this truth.

What Are Wonders?

The Hebrew word for *wonders* is *mowpheth* and means "a supernatural act which has the purpose to demonstrate the power of God."[3] It occurs 36 times in the Old Testament. One of the Greek words for wonders is *dunamis* and has, among other meanings, the sense of "a miracle through supernatural power."[4] It occurs 123 times in the New Testament. This Greek word is used in all of the following scriptures, which we will look at now:

> *But you shall receive power [**dunamis**] when the Holy Spirit has come upon you; and you shall be witnesses to Me in Jerusalem, and in all Judea and Samaria, and to the end of the earth.*
>
> —ACTS 1:8

> *Many will say to Me in that day, "Lord, Lord, have we not prophesied in Your name, cast out demons in Your name, and done many wonders [**dunamis**] in Your name?"*

And when the Sabbath had come, He began to teach in the synagogue. And many hearing Him were astonished, saying, "Where did this Man get these things? And what wisdom is this which is given to Him, that such mighty works [dunamis] are performed by His hands!"

—MARK 6:2

Woe to you, Chorazin! Woe to you, Bethsaida! For if the mighty works [dunamis] which were done in you had been done in Tyre and Sidon, they would have repented long ago, sitting in sackcloth and ashes."

—LUKE 10:13

I wrote the word *dunamis* in brackets behind each word in the Greek that is used for *wonders*. Every single time, the same Greek word is used and means "a wonder." Remember, the definition is "a miracle through supernatural power." Jesus said that when we receive the Holy Spirit it will be a miracle through a supernatural power. When we are baptized in the Holy Spirit, we are all enabled to do miracles through the supernatural power of God. We just have to learn to believe in it and activate it.

The Source of the Supernatural

There are only two sources of the supernatural: God and Satan. The motives behind these two sources are opposite. God is love, and when He does miracles, He is motivated by love. We must reject a theology that teaches that all the natural disasters and terrible things that are happening in this world are from God. We live in the age of grace where all of God's supernatural actions are motivated by love.

The devil, who is the second source of the supernatural, always has the motive of destruction. There are people who heal others supernaturally through demonic power. I have been told, "Something good happens; therefore, it cannot be the devil." I have talked to several people who have experienced physical healing that way. Without exception, the result was always devastating. Often, one pain left, but three others came. Sometimes the individual had no more physical sickness but ended up in depression or with destroyed relationships. Let me assure you that the devil only has one motive when he does something supernaturally: to harm and to destroy.

Signs Following

Jesus said that certain supernatural signs would follow those who believe the gospel. As we are told in Mark 16:17–20,

> *"And these signs will follow those who believe: In My name they will cast out demons; they will speak with new tongues; they will take up serpents; and if they drink anything deadly, it will by no means hurt them; they will lay hands on the sick, and they will recover." So then, after the Lord had spoken to them, He was received up into heaven, and sat down at the right hand of God. And they went out and preached everywhere, the Lord working with them and confirming the word through the accompanying signs. Amen.*

The word *follow* in these verses is the Greek word *parakoloutheo*, which means "to follow somebody and be constantly at their side."[5] It has its root in the Greek word *parakletos*, which is used for the Holy Spirit. He is the one who is always on our side and will never leave us. This is very important for us to understand because when Jesus told His disciples to preach the gospel, He said that these supernatural signs would follow everyone who believes.

Let us ask ourselves this question: what went wrong in church history? Remember, the Greek word for *follow* means "to be constantly at somebody's side." Jesus did not say these supernatural actions should happen occasionally through the life of some anointed person of God, which is what we, unfortunately, experience today. Jesus said that they should constantly be "at the side" of every single believer!

It is one of the great passions of my heart to see supernatural power restored in the life of every believer as a normal, everyday thing. I have made a radical decision; I will not rest, but will cry out to God with fasting and prayer until I see the glory of God through the power of the supernatural in the body of Christ.

When Jesus said, "These signs shall follow those who believe: in My name they will [do all the supernatural works mentioned in that verse]," the meaning was very clear. He did *not* mean that we should add the phrase "In the name of Jesus" at the end of a prayer. There is nothing wrong with doing this; however, the power is not in the phrase, but in what our hearts truly believe. I will explain this at greater length in a later chapter when I talk about our authority as believers. What Jesus meant was that through faith in Him, we have now become united *with Him* and are *in Him*. Therefore, our authority is *exactly the same* as His authority.

Signs and Wonders in the New Testament

The entire New Testament is filled with stories of signs and wonders. I will show you some in the following passages. It has been my deliberate choice to leave out any signs and wonders in the life of Jesus for two reasons. First, there are too many to put in this book. Second, people have argued with me too many times and said, "Well, that was Jesus, and I'm not Him." The seventy disciples, whom Jesus sent out, did extraordinary miracles, which we see in Luke 10:17: *"Then the seventy returned with joy, saying, 'Lord, even the demons are subject to us in Your name.'"*

The apostles did many outstanding miracles which we see in the following two verses:

So great fear came upon all the church and
upon all who heard these things. And
through the hands of the apostles many
signs and wonders were done among the
people. And they were all with one accord in
Solomon's Porch.

—ACTS 5:11–12

Stephen was neither an apostle nor a pastor. He was simply a deacon, yet through his life, outstanding miracles took place.

And Stephen, full of faith and power, did
great wonders and signs among the people.
—ACTS 6:8

Philip was another man through whom extraordinary signs and wonders were demonstrated, as we can read in Acts 8:6–8 and 13:

And the multitudes with one accord heeded
the things spoken by Philip, hearing and
seeing the miracles which he did. For
unclean spirits, crying with a loud voice,
came out of many who were possessed; and
many who were paralyzed and lame were
healed. And there was great joy in that city.
. . . Then Simon himself also believed; and
when he was baptized he continued with

Philip, and was amazed, seeing the miracles and signs which were done.

Endnotes

1. *Owth*, "signal," Strong's #226; http://www.studylight.org/lexicons/hebrew/hwview.cgi?n=226, accessed 15 September 2016.

2. *Sēmeîon*, "signs," Strong's #4592; http://www.studylight.org/lexicons/greek/gwview.cgi?n=4592, accessed 15 September 2016.

3. *Môphêth*, "wonder," Strong's #4159; http://www.studylight.org/lexicons/hebrew/hwview.cgi?n=4159, accessed 15 September 2016.

4. *Dunamis*, "power," Strong's #1411; http://biblehub.com/greek/1411.htm, accessed 15 September 2016.

5. *Parakoloutheó*, "to follow," Strong's #3877; http://biblehub.com/greek/3877.htm, accessed 15 September 2016.

Testimony

My name is Yvone, and I am from Lichtenstein, Germany. Our

daughter Sara was born with just part of her hipbones. The doctor that examined her told us she would never walk, and that, if she walked, it would be with great limitations. On August 2014, we asked for prayer for our Sara. Two weeks after she received prayer, we had another appointment with the doctor. When the doctor examined her, he found perfect hips. When she turned a year old, she started walking and running everywhere. Today, in February 2016, she is twenty months old, and she walks and runs perfectly well. Glory to God!

Testimony

My name is Miriam, and I live in Florida. We've been in church for six years, and for ten years, my husband and I have lived in the US. My job demands a lot from my shoulders. I felt great pain in my left shoulder, and it was about to become a serious case of bursitis. My whole arm bothered me. In a church meeting, I cried out for my healing before God. When I saw a woman being healed that night, my heart was filled with faith to receive my healing. Later in that meeting, I was invited to go to the front after a word of knowledge about the pain in my right shoulder. I stood up and went to the front. As the church prayed for me, the pain still continued. After I was prayed for three times, my shoulder still felt too heavy until suddenly I felt a pop on my shoulder. At that moment, they asked me if I felt anything. Actually, my shoulder was so light that I could not even feel it. The other day I felt some pain in my shoulder, but I declared my healing. I did it all day long. At the end of the day, I noticed I had no pain anymore.

Chapter 10

Signs and Wonders, Continued
Three Important Factors

In order for us to experience signs and wonders through our lives, we have to have three very important factors: a need, God, and a channel. *Firstly*, if you do not have a need, you do not need a miracle. Therefore, the greater and more desperate the need is, the more you need a miracle. When we think about need, we often think only about sickness. This must not be our mentality. God not only wants to heal our broken bodies, He wants to manifest Himself through signs and wonders in every need that we face in every area of our lives. Once our need is so desperate that it is beyond any human help, we have met the first condition for a miracle.

This truth applies to every area of our lives and the lives of the people around us. Do you have a desperate financial need? Then you are a candidate for supernatural provision. Do you have a desperate physical need? Then you are a candidate for supernatural healing. Do you have a desperate family need? Then you are a candidate for supernatural restoration and salvation. May I challenge you to apply this principle to every single area in your life that is in need?

Secondly, we need God. As we have already seen, there are only two sources of the supernatural: God and the devil. Since we do not want to have any miracles from the devil, there is only God left as our source—and we desperately need Him.

The questions that have to be firmly answered in our hearts are questions like these: Does God always want to do miracles for and through us? Is God good, only good, and always good? Is God the source of any pain or harm in my life? Is there any miracle that I need that God has not yet paid for through the finished work of the cross? Is God always for us, or could He be against us in certain circumstances or situations? Could my perfect relationship with God ever be broken by anything I do?

There are many more similar questions that we have to be convinced about in our hearts in order to experience the supernatural. I will not answer any of these questions here in depth as I plan to write a book about the New Covenant soon. Let me assure you, it is my own conviction that John 19:30 is the most powerful passage in the entire Bible. Jesus said on the cross, "It is finished!" There is nothing that can be added to the finished work of the cross.

Because of the finished work of the cross *alone,* God always wants to do miracles for and through us. Because of the finished work of the cross *alone,* God has proven that He is good, only good, and always good. Because of the finished work of the cross *alone,* God can never be the source of any pain or harm in my life because He put the punishment that I deserved on Christ.

Because of the finished work of the cross *alone,* every miracle that I could ever need has already been paid for. Jesus' statement "It is finished" is expressed in the original Greek in a way that is impossible to directly translate. The best way we can translate it is "It is completely completed, and nothing can be added to it." It is an action in the past that can never be changed, and it is absolute. Therefore, every single miracle that we will ever need in any area of our lives has been completely completed, absolutely paid for, and only has to be received by faith.

Because of the finished work of the cross *alone,* God can never be against us. There is nothing we can do for which God could ever reject us. When Jesus was on the cross, God was against His own Son and rejected Him so that we can be accepted forever.

Because of the finished work of the cross *alone,* God Himself has made peace with us through Jesus Christ. To have *peace with us* means to have a perfectly restored relationship. This word *peace* has its root in the medical field. At that time, when doctors set a broken bone so it would heal, *once the bone was perfectly healed together,* the doctors would say, "Now there is peace."

Our relationship with God is perfectly set together. Since this perfectly restored relationship has not taken place because of anything we have done, but only through what Jesus did, it can never again be broken. Once these questions have been firmly and positively answered in your own heart, you have met the second condition that you need for a miracle to be fulfilled.

Now let us look at the *third* factor we need in order to have a miracle: the channel. There is a big difference between the source and the channel. In our lives, God must always be the source of the supernatural; however, very rarely is He the source and the channel.

The source is that from which something originates; power is released from the source. The channel is the person or thing through which the power flows. It is more important than we realize to distinguish this point. Since God alone is the source, the source will never run dry. There are no limitations whatsoever because He is God. When I said that very rarely is God both the source and the channel, I meant that very rarely will God Himself do a miracle without involving either a human or an angelic channel.

The other important thing for us to understand is that the channel can be totally weak and even helpless as long as it is connected to the source. The channel can never take any ounce of glory for self, since the origin of the miracle is not in self. Because of our wrong way of thinking, we are constantly tempted to look to the channel for miracles instead of looking to the source. In some of my weakest moments, God has done some of the greatest miracles. At those times, I understood that I am a channel who is connected to the limitless source of the supernatural who is God.

When God does extraordinary things through me and people try to put me on a pedestal, I simply thank them and smile, but in my heart I immediately say, *"Lord, this glory is for You, not for me."* I abhor it when people try to glorify any channel which God uses, including me. We must stop glorifying channels and give the source, who is God, all the glory. Once we can grasp this, the entire body of Christ—from the weakest to the strongest member—will move in the supernatural.

Since God, as the source of the supernatural, has chosen to let His power flow through a channel, He is constantly looking for people to be these channels. As I mentioned in a previous chapter, our relationship with God is not determined but dynamic.

We are not robots; we are free human agents with a free will given by God. As you study the lives of great heroes of faith, you will discover that it was not God's sovereign choice to use them in the supernatural. Did Jesus not say that greater works than He Himself did would be done by those who believe in Him? God has already determined who will move in the supernatural. The invitation is open to every single Christian. When He said, "Those who believe in Me," He determined that anyone can be the channel of the limitless power of God. Since we have a dynamic relationship with God, we must have our minds renewed and be determined to be channels through whom these greater works can be done.

Calvin was partially right when he said that our relationship with God is *determined* and that He alone decides where and when He will do a miracle. He was wrong, however, when he said that we have no influence upon this. God has already determined, which we see in John 14:12 and Mark 16:14–20, that He always wants to do miracles through anybody who dares to be a channel.

One of Many Experiences

I have had many experiences where I, as the channel, was so ridiculously weak that God never could have done a miracle through me if I had believed that I was the source. I was once on an airplane from North Carolina to Seattle, Washington. It was a long flight that took many hours. On the airplane, I got very sick with strong diarrhea and vomiting. Throughout the flight, I had to keep running to the restroom.

When I arrived in Seattle, the pastor picked me up from the airport and took me to my hotel. He informed me that in about two hours he would pick me up to preach at his church. I had a fever, which I rarely ever get; my body was shaking; and I felt extremely weak. I called my wife to ask her for prayer and had to hang up on her to run to the bathroom to vomit.

When I arrived at the church building, the first question I asked the pastor was "What is the quickest way to get to the restroom?" I had no idea how I would make it through an hour-and-a-half of ministry without crapping my pants or vomiting. When I stepped into the pulpit and began to preach, there was a young man sitting in the front row who had his arm in a sling because of an injured shoulder. That same day he had dropped a bar with heavy weights on his shoulder.

After a few minutes of preaching, I looked at him and felt prompted to pray for a miracle. My mind kept screaming at me, *"How can you pray for his healing when you are sick? How do you think your faith will work for him when it doesn't even work for you? Look how sick you are. God doesn't want to heal you; what makes you think He wants to heal him?"*

These and many other such questions raced through my mind. I never fought any of these questions, which I have learned is one of the secrets to live in the supernatural. You don't fight negative thoughts; you simply ignore them, smile, and make a choice to think right thoughts.

I stopped preaching, stepped down from the platform, and walked up to the young man thinking, "I am not the source; I am only the channel." When I reached him, I commanded every injury in that shoulder to be gone instantly. I told him to take his arm out of the sling and raise it high. He was completely healed and was playing the drums in the next service.

This truth has to penetrate our hearts. The source has limitless power and desires constantly to demonstrate it, but it will not do so without willing channels. God will not sovereignly choose the channels, as many falsely believe. He has already chosen for His power to flow through anybody who is a willing channel when He said, *"He who believes in Me, the works that I do he will do also; and greater works than these he will do, because I go to My Father"* (John 14:12).

As we consider these three things which we need for a miracle—a need, God, and a channel, we have to understand that the first two are constantly present, but the third is so often missing. Everywhere we go there are so many needs. I travel every week to many nations and am daily confronted with the overwhelming needs of many people who have all kinds of physical, emotional, material, and spiritual needs.

Often these needs cannot be met with any human resource; God alone can do that. There are sicknesses which the doctors have no answer for, broken and destroyed souls of abused children, and wounded hearts from broken relationships. We could go on and on about all the terrible and diverse needs we are confronted with every single day.

Why are there so few miracles today? Maybe you think that there are many miracles—but in relation to the countless needs, they seem very few.

So often we look for a reason for a a lack of miracles, as well as for anything else that we don't experience, in the wrong place—God. God surely is not the reason for any lack of miracles; He has already determined that He desperately wants to express His love and power to a broken world.

Since the first and second things we need for a miracle are always present, the problem has to lie with the third thing we need—the channel. God is lacking willing and surrendered channels who have made a decision to risk it all for His glory, to step out in radical faith, and to not worry about their glory or their reputation. As these channels become available to God, miracles will be seen everywhere because needs and God are everywhere.

God has used me to be a channel of His supernatural power in airplanes, shopping malls, on the street, and every place you can imagine. People who don't really know me think that God only uses me in meetings where I preach. God desires to have available channels every single place where there is a need.

Can you imagine what would happen if this book would stir people to become available channels for God's supernatural power? This power is an expression of His deep love for people all over the world. Can you imagine this book inspiring people to become these channels on the streets, in the schools, in their homes, at their work places, and in all the public places we go and find needs? God is already there, desperately looking for available channels. It is my heart's cry that this will take place before Christ returns. We will transform our homes, cities, and nations.

I challenge you to pause right here and begin to pray. Ask the Holy Spirit to help you to become a totally surrendered and available channel of His deep love, which will be expressed through His supernatural power. Make a decision of total and radical surrender to live a life of radical faith. You are not the source; you are just a channel. God Himself is the source. He will not use you until you decide that you will be the channel that He has been looking for. Pray a prayer of total surrender and availability. Begin to cry out to God for the needs around you and tell Him in your own words something like this, "Here I am, Lord; use me, flow through me, heal through me, transform through me . . ."

The devil will tempt you to look at your own weaknesses, and he will try to stop you with all sorts of lies. Simply ignore him and tell God that you are so glad that He is the source and you are just the channel.

The Element of Faith

We can only be channels of the supernatural power of God if we live a radical life of faith. That is clearly demonstrated throughout the entire Bible. One of the problems we have is that we would like to have the blessings of Abraham with the faith of Thomas. We want God to show us His supernatural power and then we will surely believe, as Thomas did when he said, "I will not believe until I see." Abraham, on the other hand, believed before he had any sign that Sarah was pregnant or he was a father.

Let me assure you, miracles do not create faith. If they did, the people of Israel would have surely entered the Promised Land because they saw miracles all the time while in the wilderness. Their deliverance from Egypt was supernatural. Crossing the Red Sea was supernatural. The cloud by day and fire by night was supernatural. Water out of the rock was supernatural, as was food flying down from heaven. Yet, when they stood at the border of the Promised Land, they did not enter it because of unbelief.

The only means of transport for the supernatural power of God to flow from its source through the channels to the people in need is radical faith. I encourage you to read my book *Faith* in which I teach you how to become a channel of the supernatural.

Testimony

My name is Mônica, and I am from Silvânia, Brazil. In 2014, when I was 29 years old, I found out I had a disease that runs in my family. This disease (polycystic kidney disease) paralyzes the kidneys. To make matters worse, this disease made my kidneys grow. While a normal kidney would be 11 cm long, mine was already 18 cm. It caused a lot of pain and discomfort. Even with this pain, I participated in a conference. While

I was there, the pain grew intense, and I had to take some medications, but they did not work. When the pastor started preaching, I was already crying desperately because it really hurt. I started praying and crying out for the healing of the Lord in my life. The answer was immediate. Hallelujah! The pastor said God would heal a woman who was desperate because of a disease. I started feeling like a fire was burning in the region of my kidneys. I was crying and thanking the Lord while the pastor prayed when I heard him say, "The Lord healed your kidney!" I was amazed and thankful. Thank You, Jesus! All I am is for Your praise! My appointments with the doctor (nephrologist) were usually every six months, but after the exams showed that my kidneys were working perfectly well, I only went to the doctor once a year. Jesus Christ healed me for His honor and glory. All honor and glory shall be given to our Lord Jesus Christ!

Chapter 11

Women and the Supernatural

I am persuaded that women have an advantage over men when it comes to living a supernatural lifestyle. Maybe you wonder how I can come to such a conclusion—and you might disagree with me. I have not come to this conclusion because women move in the supernatural more than men.

Women are supposed to move equally or more than men in the supernatural because, naturally speaking, it is easier for them than for men. Sadly, few women know this and use their advantage. I hope that through these next chapters I can inspire and release every woman to live a supernatural lifestyle. I also do hope that as this happens it will stir every man to a godly jealousy so that they will also live a supernatural lifestyle.

The Heart of Compassion

When Jesus healed the sick and moved in the supernatural, He did so because He was driven by compassion. Look at these following verses, and you will see a direct connection between compassion and the supernatural in the life of Jesus. Notice that these verses are not just speaking about healing, but also about multiplying food because He had compassion on those who were hungry.

> *And when Jesus went out He saw a great multitude; and He was moved with compassion for them, and healed their sick.*
> —MATTHEW 14:14

> *Now Jesus called His disciples to Himself and said, "I have compassion on the multitude, because they have now continued with Me three days and have nothing to eat. And I do not want to send them away hungry, lest they faint on the way."*
> —MATTHEW 15:32

> *So Jesus had compassion and touched their eyes. And immediately their eyes received sight, and they followed Him.*
> —MATTHEW 20:34

> *Then Jesus, moved with compassion, stretched out His hand and touched him, and said to him, "I am willing; be cleansed."*

—MARK 1:41

However, Jesus did not permit him, but said to him, "Go home to your friends, and tell them what great things the Lord has done for you, and how He has had compassion on you."

—MARK 5:19

Women are naturally much more compassionate than men. Therefore, they should have an inclination to move in the supernatural. The reason why Jesus did all these miracles was because compassion drove Him to do so. Men are often motivated by many different things when they desire to see the supernatural power of God. Some of these motives are legitimate; others are not. Usually passion is a stronger motive in men than compassion is. I believe this should not be so. Among the different motives men have, compassion is usually not uppermost on the list. It certainly was in the life of Jesus though.

When a child is hurt and in pain, it is naturally inclined to run to mommy and not daddy because mom has a heart of compassion. In many cultures, this is seen as a weakness when moms are very compassionate with boys who hurt themselves because boys are supposed to be "tough" and cuddling them will take away from their "toughness" somehow, they imagine. Let me remind you that the compassion in the heart of Jesus was what moved Him to perform miracles.

Since childhood, I have had a deep desire to see the supernatural power of God, especially in the area of healing. In 1982, I went to a special conference in England. For quite a while beforehand, I had been fasting and praying for God to use me in healing. Nobody knew about that—only God and me. My motive was, among others things, a passion for the kingdom of God and the Word of God. While I was at that conference in a strange country, a preacher who had never seen me before had a word of knowledge.

There were probably about 700 to 800 people in that meeting. The preacher said that there was a young man in the congregation who had been desperately crying out to God to be used in miracles. God would not respond to this prayer until the motive changed. The preacher continued to say that only as this young man had a heart of compassion for the sick, which Jesus Himself had, would God use Him in miracles. You can imagine that word of knowledge hit me in the center of my heart.

Let me illustrate the difference between the more passionate nature of men and the more compassionate nature of women with an experience my wife and I had just recently. We were ministering in another city when a pastor was driving us back to our accommodation. We passed by a woman who was beating a small child on the sidewalk. The pastor expressed his shock verbally, drawing our attention to the scene. It was very interesting to see the different reactions in my wife and this pastor. While my wife felt compassion for the child, the pastor felt anger (passion) against the abusive woman.

Ladies, let me encourage you: when you feel compassion regarding any desperate situation that you face, you should understand it as an invitation from God to experience the supernatural. Let me draw your attention back to the aforementioned verses. When Jesus felt compassion because the people were hungry, it drove Him to do a miracle by multiplying food. When He felt compassion for sick people, it drove Him to perform miracles of healings. His motives were not passion, but compassion.

This is why I believe women naturally have an advantage over men. Women just have not learned how to use their compassionate hearts to their own advantage regarding the supernatural. Every woman simply needs to understand that each time her heart breaks with compassion, it is an invitation from God to believe in the supernatural and experience a miracle.

Instead of letting your natural mother-instinct control you, let the supernatural instinct of God drive you to bring the supernatural power of God from heaven to earth. I do not want to say that your natural mother-instinct is something bad; however, if it limits you to a merely natural reaction instead of a supernatural reaction, I believe you have missed the true purpose of having a heart of compassion.

When you see the many needs around you, do not allow your heart of compassion to frustrate you; do not try to fix the problems in the natural. Look at it as a blessing of God as well as a great advantage that you have over men. Reach out in faith and let it drive you to develop a supernatural lifestyle.

The Healing of My Son

When our younger son was about six months old, he became very sick. The doctors discovered an under-developed lung and severe laryngitis. He was rushed to the hospital and then for the following seven years suffered greatly. Medically speaking, there was no hope for him. My wife and I spent many nights next to his bed when he was struggling to breathe and survive. Hundreds of prayers went up on his behalf during those long years.

One night, he stood next to our bed as he had done so many times before. He struggled for breath and desperately needed help. I got out of bed, took him back to his bed, and told him to wait for me as I got the inhaler with strong medication and cortisone for him. As I went to the kitchen to prepare his medication, I had an overwhelming experience with God. I felt a pain and compassion in my heart that was too deep and strong to even find words to express. I collapsed on the floor and cried out in prayer motivated by nothing but the deepest compassion I had ever experienced in my life.

It was not a father's compassion for a son, but God's own compassionate heart that I felt. When I got up from my knees, I went to check on my son who was peacefully asleep and instantly healed. Nineteen years later, he is still enjoying the fruit of that compassionate prayer which brought the supernatural power of God into his life.

Testimony

Llana is an eight-year-old girl who could only see through glasses. When she received prayer in Londrina, Brazil, she was completely healed. Thanks to the Lord, she does not need glasses anymore—either to see close or to see far away. All glory to God!

Testimony

I had a disease in the bone of my gum and was scheduled to go for surgery. A day before the surgery, I went to a church service, and the pastor said people would be healed. He knew it because God told him. The first problem he mentioned was of a person who had a disease in the bones of the mouth. Everything he said was exactly what I had, so I stood up. He told me that the Lord was healing me at that very moment, and I took my blessing. I never felt anything again, and I did not have to have surgery. To this day, I am fine, in the name of Jesus. Amen!

Chapter 12

Women and Sensitivity

Women are not only naturally more compassionate than men; they are also naturally more sensitive. Men often do not want to face this truth, but it cannot be denied. Did you know that there are more female Christians than male? I believe the reason for this is that women are more sensitive than men and therefore respond more easily to the drawing of the Holy Spirit. I am not saying that men are insensitive, but I do say that, naturally speaking, women are more inclined to being sensitive than men are.

Sensitivity is a precious God-given gift which women have. They feel things so much more quickly and deeply than most men do. I want to encourage every woman reading this book not to be afraid to be sensitive or consider it a weakness in any way. Embrace this as a precious gift from God.

Sensitivity is how strongly and how deeply we feel things. The issue is never the actual sensitivity, but the application of it. When you feel things deeply, let your emotions control your choices in a negative way, and make irrational decisions, you have applied your sensitivity wrongly. On the other hand, when you feel things strongly and deeply and allow God to use this sensitivity to drive you to live a supernatural lifestyle, you have correctly applied sensitivity.

When God began to use me in the prophetic and the supernatural, I had to learn to become very sensitive to the Holy Spirit. Often men consider sensitivity to be a weakness. I believe it is one of the greatest strengths that anybody can have. Because women are naturally more sensitive, they have an advantage over men when it comes to living in the supernatural.

When the Lord taught me how to be sensitive, it was a very painful learning process. I remember the day my wife told me that I was in touch with my feminine side. What she meant as a compliment felt offensive to me until she explained to me how good that was. Ladies, you should be thankful to God for this sensitivity that He naturally built inside of you.

Sensitivity and the Supernatural

Sensitivity is much more important when it comes to living a supernatural lifestyle than we realize. Jesus Himself was very sensitive in every way. He was sensitive to the voice of His Father, as well as the needs of the people.

Scripture is clear that the husband is the head of the wife. Having said that, I do believe that we men might have saved ourselves many troubles and the kingdom of God might have advanced much faster if we had been more humble and listened to the sensitive hearts of our wives more often.

I can already see the stones come flying from men who are reading these lines. I am not afraid to be stoned for saying what I believe. The stones will only fly from men who are so insecure that they have to control women out of their insecurity. If men are secure in who they are in Christ and encourage women to fulfill their God-given purpose, then we can all work together and see the supernatural power of the kingdom of God released in every area of our lives.

How many women have prayed and interceded because their sensitive hearts felt a need? As they did so, God did many outstanding things in response to those prayers. If women can learn to embrace their sensitivity as a God-given gift and an invitation from God to walk in the supernatural, they will understand that in this area they have an advantage over men.

I believe that before Jesus returns we will see a church that moves in power and authority. There will be an explosion of the supernatural among all the members of the body of Christ. Among other things, God is going to use women to help bring this about. As women use their God-given sensitivity to tap into the powers of the kingdom of God by faith and change difficult situations, many men will also be stirred up to live a life of the supernatural.

The Role of the Holy Spirit

In order to understand this truth of sensitivity in relation to the supernatural, we must understand the role of the Holy Spirit. Nothing significantly supernatural takes place without the Trinity working together in perfect unity and harmony. The importance of the relationship of the Trinity is clearly seen throughout Scripture. If we want to be used by God in the supernatural, we must live in a right relationship with all three parts of the Godhead (Father, Son, and Holy Spirit).

In order to interpret the Bible correctly, we need to apply the law of first mention, which says that in order to understand the Bible correctly on any given subject we have to locate where that subject is first mentioned in Scripture. Let us look at where the supernatural is mentioned in the Bible for the very first time. We are told in Genesis 1:1–3,

> *In the beginning God created the heavens and the earth. The earth was without form, and void; and darkness was on the face of the deep. And the Spirit of God was hovering over the face of the waters. Then God said, "Let there be light"; and there was light.*

Here we see the three parts of the Godhead mentioned for the first time, as well as the first miracle, which was creation. Father, Son, and Holy Spirit worked harmoniously together to bring about the first supernatural act of God. God spoke while the Spirit of God was hovering over the face of the waters, waiting to bring to pass what the Father wanted.

Maybe you are wondering where Jesus is mentioned here. John 1:1–2 tells us, *"In the beginning was the Word and the Word was with God, and the Word was God. He was in the beginning with God."* Jesus was the Word of God. When God spoke, He released Jesus, who was the Word, to become active in creation. As we look at the Bible as a whole, it is not hard to find out that the creation was completed by all three parts of the Godhead. When God said, "Let there be light," Jesus became involved in creation because He is the Word of God. We are told in Colossians 1:15–16 that it was Jesus Himself who created all things:

> *He is the image of the invisible God, the firstborn over all creation.* ***For by Him all things were created*** *that are in heaven and that are on earth, visible and invisible, whether thrones or dominions or principalities or powers. All things were created through Him and for Him.* (Empasis mine)

We can only understand the first three verses in Genesis if we interpret them by the Bible as a whole. In Genesis, it seems like God the Father alone created the world while Colossians tells us that it was Jesus who created the world. Psalm 33:6 tells us, *"By the word of the LORD the heavens were made, and all the host of them by the breath of His mouth."* The word for *breath* is the word that is used for the Holy Spirit. There are no miracles without the Father, Son, and the Holy Spirit working together.

What does this have to do with a chapter especially for women? Since it is not only the Father and the Son Jesus perfoming miracles, but also the Holy Spirit, only people who have learned to be sensitive to the Holy Spirit can move in the supernatural. Since women are naturallymore sensitve, they can more easily relate to the Holy Spirit and therefore live a life of the supernatural.

We can see this same principle of the supernatural only happening when the Trinity works together in Acts 10:38:

> . . . *how God anointed Jesus of Nazareth with the **Holy Spirit** and with power, who went about doing good and healing all who were oppressed by the devil, for God was with Him.* (Emphasis mine)

God desperately wanted to do miracles and heal the people because He passionately loved them. Jesus was the channel through whom He chose to show His supernatural power. But Jesus could not do it without the anointing of the Holy Spirit. The more sensitive you are to the Holy Spirit, the more He can use you as a channel to bring the supernatural power of God to the people.

Testimony

My name is Hayam Chandra. Three months before going to a conference, I had surgery on my wisdom tooth (third molar) because it was in the wrong position and my bone went out of place. As I opened my mouth, it really hurt, and I couldn't feel my bone moving. When the pastor said that he wanted to pray for a person who had been through a surgery exactly three months before that day, a sister reminded me of my surgery, so I stood up. I laid my hands where it hurt, and I really believed for my healing. At the moment, a song started playing, the Holy Spirit came, and I started speaking in tongues. I opened my mouth, and I felt no pain. Tears started falling down my cheeks because I felt such a powerful glory of the Lord God.

Testimony

My name is Dines. I participated in a conference in Macapa, Brazil, and I was really moved by the account of Jesus healing with the power and authority of the Holy Spirit. There was a moment in which the people who wanted to be healed were called to the front. I had suffered a car accident in which my car rolled over five times. My back and my hip were damaged, and I felt strong pain in my legs and couldn't walk well. At that moment, God told me He would use that pastor to heal me and that I should go where he was. That moved me so much that I started shaking in a supernatural way. When the pastor passed by me, I told him what God had told me. He asked me if I believed that. I said I did, and he started praying with me. The Holy Spirit touched me, and I stood up. I was healed for the honor and glory of God. Amen!

Chapter 13

Women Love Communion

Communion is an important part of the supernatural. In fact, without communion we cannot live a life of the miraculous. Women are naturally much more inclined to desire communion. Therefore, they have another advantage over men regarding living a life in the supernatural.

Two meanings of the word *communion* are "fellowship" and "intimacy." It is naturally much easier for women to intimately share their hearts with one another than it is for men to do so. Men are naturally much more superficial in their relationships with one another. Typically, if you ask a man how he is, he will say, "I'm fine," and that is the end of the conversation. When women ask each other the same question, it often opens up a long conversation about things that are on their hearts. Women naturally desire fellowship and communion; therefore, it is easier for them to practice this fellowship with the Holy Spirit and so tap into the supernatural power of God.

For a long time, I have been pondering and meditating on 2 Corinthians 13:14: *"The grace of the Lord Jesus Christ, and the love of God, and the communion of the Holy Spirit be with you all. Amen."* As we look at this scripture we see another secret for a supernatural lifestyle hidden here. I will explain this secret in more detail, but in simple words, the secret involves the connection between the love of God, the grace of Jesus, and the fellowship of the Holy Spirit. Once again, the Trinity works together in perfect harmony and unity.

The first thing we see is the love of God. He looks at you with His eyes of love and deeply desires to bless you abundantly—supernaturally releasing all of the heavenly gifts into your life. Because we had all fallen short, broken the law of God, and were not worthy to have *all* the abundance of God's blessing supernaturally brought to us, God had to find a way to do so.

This verse talks about the grace of the Lord Jesus. What God desired to give to us but could not because we were lawbreakers, Jesus made possible by keeping the law for us. One of the definitions of *grace* is "unmerited favor." Through His death and resurrection, Jesus Christ suffered all the punishment and consequences which we should have received for our sin so that now we can receive His grace (favor). We are now in a position to receive everything which the love of God desires to give to us.

To put this in simple words, God, in His passionate love, wanted to bless us but could not because His righteous nature had to punish us for our sins. Jesus paid for everything that God desired to give us; therefore, it is now legally ours.

In this single verse (2 Cor. 13:14), where we see the Trinity working together again, the communion of the Holy Spirit is also mentioned. This verse says that the communion of the Holy Spirit shall be with us. It is the Holy Spirit that opens the treasure chest of heaven and brings the supernatural into our lives. Since He is the one who does it, we can only experience it if we live in communion with Him.

Once again, women naturallly have an advantage over men. One of the meanings of *communion* is "fellowship," which women love. Men are much more goal- and task-oriented than women are. Although women can successfully work toward and achieve great goals, fellowship is an important part of their lives in achieving those goals. Since it is through the communion of the Holy Spirit that we work together with Him in perfect partnership, we must make sure that we learn how to live in this communion.

As you learn to walk in communion and fellowship with the Holy Spirit, you will quickly begin to experience the supernatural. Here is what the fellowship of the Holy Spirit will bring to your life:

> *He gives you power.* We are told in Acts 1:8 that with the Holy Spirit we will receive power: *"But you shall receive power when the Holy Spirit has come upon you."* The more we learn to fellowship with the Holy Spirit, the more that the power that we have already received by being baptized in Him will be released through our lives.
>
> *He gives you wisdom and revelation.* The Holy Spirit is also called the Spirit of wisdom and revelation. In the measure

that you learn to fellowship and have intimate communion with Him, His wisdom will be seen in your life.

He teaches you how to apply the truth of the Word of God. Without the Holy Spirit, the Word of God is nothing but dead letters that will not help but harm us. We are told in Second Corinthians 3:6, *"Who also made us sufficient as ministers of the new covenant, not of the letter but of the Spirit; for the letter kills, but the Spirit gives life."* Since it is the Holy Spirit who enables us to understand the Bible in the light of the New Covenant, we desperately need to walk in communion with Him.

He tells us what Jesus could not tell His disciples. When I first discovered the following verses, I got so excited. John 16:12–13 tells us, *"I still have many things to say to you, but you cannot bear them now. However, when He, the Spirit of truth, has come, He will guide you into all truth; for He will not speak on His own authority, but whatever He hears He will speak; and He will tell you things to come."*

There were many things that Jesus never told His disciples because He was unable to do so at that time. Jesus promised that it would be the Holy Spirit who would communicate these things to them. For a long time, I purposely spent a lot of time in fellowship with the Holy Spirit, asking Him to tell me the things which Jesus could not tell His disciples. It is in communion with Him that these secrets will be made known to us. Since He is the one who brings the supernatural into our lives and communion is one of the

ways we relate with Him,
women should be glad that
they have this advantage with
their natural love of
communion.

He brings us His gifts. The Bible talks a
lot about the gifts of the
Spirit. That is another thing
that women naturally love
much more than men. In any
country I have ever visited, I
have noticed that women love
to receive and give gifts. The
Holy Spirit desires to share
His gifts with us. He delights
when we also desire His gifts.
Ladies, use your natural desire
for gifts to draw close to the
Holy Spirit and tell Him that
you constantly want His gifts.
By doing so, the supernatural
will become a natural part of
your life.

Ignoring and Abusing

The Holy Spirit is the most ignored and abused
person of the Godhead. The church at large relates

to God the Father and to God the Son, but very little to God the Holy Spirit. The Holy Spirit is a person and desires to live in a deep, intimate relationship with us. Without relating to Him on this intimate level, we can never live a consistent life of the supernatural. Women's need for intimacy is much greater than men's. They suffer so much more than men do when they are ignored.

The Holy Spirit does not like to be ignored, and women should naturally understand how He feels when He is ignored. This can help you to relate to Him on a daily basis and experience His supernatural power. Although we just said that He desires to give His gifts to us, which is a biblical truth, He does not want to be abused.

Every woman desires to be loved simply for who she is and not for what she has or does. Being loved and accepted simply for who she is will give her a sense of love and value. Since women understand this better than men, they are able to relate personally and intimately with the Holy Spirit without abusing Him and using Him just for His gifts.

I will never forget the moment when I said to the Holy Spirit, "Holy Spirit, I really want you to be my very best friend." He quickly replied, "I am, but I also want you to be My very best friend." For a long time, I pondered these words and asked Him to teach me what that means. It has to do with sensitivity, loyalty, friendship, and communion.

Women are so much better at these things than men are, which gives them an advantage when we talk about living in the supernatural. They just need to learn how special these attributes are that God has given them and direct them into a deep love-relationship with the Holy Spirit. As they do, they will become powerful channels of the Holy Spirit.

Grieving the Holy Spirit

Since the relationship with the Holy Spirit is key to experiencing the supernatural, we must make sure that we do not grieve Him. He is gentle, tender, and kind. We are told in Ephesians 4:30 that we must not grieve Him: *"And do not grieve the Holy Spirit of God, by whom you were sealed for the day of redemption."* *To grieve* means "to offend, make sad or sorrowful." The question that many Christians have is "How can He be grieved?" The Bible does not give much teaching about it, but from the context, we can easily find out what it means. Let us look at the context and see what we can learn.

> *Let no corrupt word proceed out of your mouth, but what is good for necessary edification, that it may impart grace to the hearers. And do not grieve the Holy Spirit of God,* **by whom you were sealed** *for the day of redemption. Let all bitterness, wrath, anger, clamor, and evil speaking be put away from you, with all malice. And be kind to one another, tenderhearted, forgiving one another, even as God in Christ forgave you.* (Emphasis mine)
> —EPHESIANS 4:29–32

As we look at verse 29 and the verses that follow it, we can clearly see what grieves Him. Verse 29 tells us that we shall not speak anything corrupt or critical, but only what gives grace to the people who hear us. It immediately tells us not to grieve the Holy Spirit, *by whom we were sealed* for the day of redemption. The same Holy Spirit who sealed us for the day of redemption also sealed every other brother and sister in Christ. Every time we criticize them or speak against them, the Holy Spirit is grieved.

The verses that follow tell us not to be angry, bitter, or say anything negative toward each other. Then we are told to be kind, tenderhearted, and forgiving. Every time we criticize, are unkind, or unforgiving, we grieve the Holy Spirit. We are told in Romans 5:5 that the Holy Spirit has brought God's love into our hearts *"because the love of God has been poured out in our hearts by the Holy Spirit who was given to us."* Since the love of God was given to us by no one other than the Holy Spirit and every one of our Christian brothers is sealed by no one other than the Holy Spirit, He is grieved when we do not walk in perfect love toward our brothers and sisters.

Testimony

My name is Maria Luana, and I am 24. Some time ago I started feeling breast pain, and as I touched my breast, I could feel a lump. I went to the doctor, and he ordered an ultrasound of my breasts. I then went to a specialist, and he said it was a node. Because the quality of the exam result was poor, he examined me and found three nodes—one in one breast and two in the other. I cried a lot because he said there was no medicine for that and that the solution would be surgery. I could not have surgery because of my age, so I was told to repeat the exams every three months. If the node did not grow, I could have exams done every six months or once a year until I could be operated on. If the node grew, I had to do a biopsy. I was desperate because of similar cases I knew about and because the exams were very expensive. But, glory to God, I participated in a conference in Macapá, Brazil. In this conference, the pastor called people to the front who had problems as I did. I raised my hand to receive some prayer, and when I noticed I was the only one receiving that prayer, I felt that God really wanted to heal me. After prayer, there were no more nodes in my breasts; I was completely healed.

Chapter 14

Women—Raising a Supernatural Generation

The Great Plan of God and the Devil's Strategy

I believe that we live in the last days before Jesus is coming back. But before He will return, He will give us a great harvest of souls. One of His important strategies, which He will use to accomplish this great harvest, involves the children.

In history, we see something very interesting. Twice before a world-changing historic event happened, the devil planned the strategic destruction of the children. We first see this in Exodus 1:15–16 when God planned to deliver His people out of Egypt in order to set them free from slavery and have a people separated for Him. God used Moses to fulfill His amazing purpose, but the devil wanted to strategically stop God's plan:

Then the king of Egypt spoke to the Hebrew midwives, of whom the name of one was Shiphrah and the name of the other Puah; and he said, "When you do the duties of a midwife for the Hebrew women, and see them on the birthstools, if it is a son, then you shall kill him; but if it is a daughter, then she shall live."

But God did not allow the plan of the enemy to come to pass and saved Moses, who should have been killed, in order to fulfill God's amazing plan. Moses was saved as a child and became a man who moved powerfully in the supernatural. We read this beautiful story of God's amazing deliverance of Moses in Exodus 2:1–10:

And a man of the house of Levi went and took as wife a daughter of Levi. So the woman conceived and bore a son. And when she saw that he was a beautiful child, she hid him three months. But when she could no longer hide him, she took an ark of bulrushes for him, daubed it with asphalt and pitch, put the child in it, and laid it in the reeds by the river's bank. And his sister stood afar off, to know what would be done to him. Then the daughter of Pharaoh came down to bathe at the river. And her

maidens walked along the riverside; and
when she saw the ark among the reeds, she
sent her maid to get it. And when she had
opened it, she saw the child, and behold, the
baby wept. So she had compassion on him,
and said, "This is one of the Hebrews'
children." Then his sister said to Pharaoh's
daughter, "Shall I go and call a nurse for
you from the Hebrew women, that she may
nurse the child for you?" And Pharaoh's
daughter said to her, "Go." So the maiden
went and called the child's mother. Then
Pharaoh's daughter said to her, "Take this
child away and nurse him for me, and I will
give you your wages." So the woman took
the child and nursed him. And the child
grew, and she brought him to Pharaoh's
daughter, and he became her son. So she
called his name Moses, saying, "Because I
drew him out of the water."

Of course, the salvation of Moses was not just about God sparing Moses' life; it was also for the higher purpose of God. This is so important to understand as God's bigger purpose is what we need to see, especially when we work with children. Through the salvation of Moses, whom the devil had planned to kill, God delivered and saved the nation of Israel with signs and wonders and a demonstration of the supernatural power of God. It is from the nation of Israel, which God so powerfully delivered, that our Savior Jesus was born. Who would have thought that this child Moses was so important in the purposes of God? You never know what God will do through the children that you are willing to raise in a supernatural lifestyle.

Let us now move forward about 1500 years to the birth of Jesus. Again, this was a world-changing, major historic event planned by God. Through the birth of Jesus, a great deliverance would come to all people from the bondage of sin. God's plan was to reconcile the world to Himself through Jesus. But again, the devil strategically planned to stop this. We know from the Bible that at the birth of Jesus, there was a major attack of the devil against children. In Matthew 2:16, we read,

> *Then Herod, when he saw that he was deceived by the wise men, was exceedingly angry; and he sent forth and put to death all the male children who were in Bethlehem and in all its districts, from two years old and under, according to the time which he had determined from the wise men.*

In His amazing power and wisdom, God was determined to fulfill His great plan and did not allow Jesus to be killed as a child. However, many children were killed, just as they were at the time of the birth of Moses.

Today we see the same strategic plan of the devil. God has planned another amazingly powerful move; He has planned to use the children to bring in a great harvest. He is raising up a generation that will fulfill His great purpose for the last days before the return of His Son Jesus. These are the children you work with today. They will live in a simple, radical, childlike faith; release signs and wonders to demonstrate God's love; move in the supernatural; and destroy the works of satan.

This is the reason why we see such a terrible satanic attack and destruction upon the lives of the children. There are more children's lives being endangered and destroyed today than ever before. I believe that through the destruction of families, drugs, child sex slavery, abuse, the legal killing of innocent babies before they are born, and the strategic destruction of them through educational programs, the devil has once again targeted our children in order to stop the move of God.

God's Outstanding Victory

I was never planned. My parents never wanted me, but God did. The devil tried to destroy my life too, but God did not permit it. I tried to kill myself three times as a child, and had several close-to-death experiences, but God in His sovereign power kept my life safe from the plan of the devil so that I could be part of what He is doing in these last days. I fully understand that He did not just save and deliver me for my own purpose, but for the great purpose that He has had since before the foundation of the world.

We see that with Moses and Jesus, even though the devil had planned a major destruction upon the children, God brought His outstanding victory and so fulfilled His prophetic purpose on the earth. Both Moses and Jesus were not only deliverers of God's people, but they also moved in the supernatural and demonstrated God's great love through signs and wonders.

Just as the devil tried to kill Moses and Jesus in order to stop the major victory which they were destined to bring, so the devil is trying to destroy our children because they are a generation of the supernatural. He is doing everything he can to destroy the lives of the children because he knows their prophetic purpose. But God will bring His outstanding victory and save, deliver, equip, and restore the children in order to bring in an amazing harvest. You and I can be a part of this wonderful work.

Our Role

The important questions are "What is our role in this work? How can we equip our children for their prophetic purpose?" Of course, before you can teach anything, you yourself have to live it. You cannot teach children something by words only; it must be taught by example. Here are important ways to teach and release them in their prophetic purpose:

Believe in their calling.
We must never see children as a burden or hard work. It is not easy to work with children. We must understand that one of the greatest privileges anybody can have is to serve God. By serving the children, we serve

God and His prophetic purpose in these last days. We have to firmly believe in their calling and see them the way God sees them—as a generation of prophetic people. Keep telling them that they are called by God to fulfill a great purpose. Continue to confess and declare that they are called to be a prophetic generation. My model is always Jesus, never Paul, Peter, Moses, Elijah, David, or any human being from the past or in the present. I am not a disciple of men, but I am a disciple of Jesus. When I look at how Jesus responded to the children, I get so excited because of the depth in His words. Mark 10:14 says, "But when Jesus saw it, He was greatly displeased and said to them, 'Let the little children come to Me, and do not forbid them; for of such is the kingdom of God.'" Let us connect this passage with what we said in the chapter about the kingdom of God. We saw that the kingdom of God is power. This is the reason why Jesus was greatly displeased when the disciples did not want the mothers to bring the children to Him. He told the disciples that the kingdom is for these children. In other words, He said that the (kingdom) power belonged to them. These children are called and destined to experience and express the supernatural power in their lives. We must believe in this truth with all of our hearts.

Encourage them to believe in the supernatural.

God wants to use our children to prophesy, heal the sick, and walk in the supernatural. They have a simple, childlike faith. Constantly encourage them to believe God for extraordinary things. Don't see them as children; see them as the ones to whom the kingdom belongs, just as Jesus said. Teach them not to react in the natural, but to always be open for a miracle.

Teach them that God is supernatural, and this is the most normal thing for us to believe. Make the miracles of the Bible come alive to them. Constantly challenge them to pray for miracles, and be confident that God will always respond to children's hearts of faith. Constantly discourage unbelief in them; teach them to push out all boundaries of limitation because if they believe, there are no limitations (Mark 9:23).

Create a hunger for God's Word in their lives.

Make the Word of God come alive to them. When I was in a children's cell group as a child, our teacher made the Word of God come alive so that I had a desperate desire to know the Bible. I was so hungry to know more of the Bible that I began to read it at a very young age. To this day, I have a deep love for the Bible. People who move in the supernatural know the Word of God, hear His voice, and do the Word of God. But they must first learn to hear His voice through the Bible.

Love them honestly and passionately.

You can never fool children. Their spirits are so wide open and sensitive. They will know if you work with them only because it is an obligation or because you truly, passionately love them. As you truly love them, their hearts will be open to receive from you. Always remember that you are an instrument in God's hands to prepare and equip this generation that the devil is so desperately trying to destroy because he is afraid of the great purpose of God. If you find it hard to truly love them, in my book *Love,* I show you how to walk in perfect love.

It is my prayer and desire that we can fulfill the desire of God's heart and raise and equip this army of prophetic children who will take this nation for Jesus.

Testimony

My name is Venis. I suffered for more than 12 years from a disease. Every hospital I went to could not discover what disease it was. They did all kinds of exams, but they found nothing. I felt strong and constant pain; I could barely get up, and sometimes I came back home from work crying because I couldn't work well. My whole body hurt, mainly my back and my neck. In a conference at Videira Taguatinga, Brazil, a pastor was preaching about faith, and I felt something in my heart. At the end of the preaching, he made an appeal for healing and prophesied. He said that Jesus wanted to heal people who were going through hard times and who had suffered from pain in the body for over ten years. It testified in my heart and in my spirit that it was my opportunity to receive my healing. Soon, I remembered the woman in the Bible who bled. All she had to do was touch Jesus to be healed. At that very moment, I went straight to the place where the pastor was. I was not afraid or ashamed, and the pastor laid his hand on me and prayed for me. When he prayed for me the third time, full of faith, he jumped and hit both hands on my back. That was when I felt the power of God inside of me, and the disease went out. I was healed for the honor and glory of Lord Jesus. Amen!

Testimony

My name is Alam. I had a broken finger. I participated in a conference where I experienced a miracle. The pastor prayed for those who were sick and for those with broken joints. I had a lot of faith, and I laid my hand where it was broken. I felt my hands tingling a lot, getting hotter and sweating. Then, the pastor told us to take the hand away from the broken place and check if it still hurt. I opened and closed my hand, and there was no pain. I could see I was healed.

Chapter 15

Our Authority

As Christians, we have an incredible authority which we can only use if we understand and believe it. It makes no difference how much authority we have if we never use it. After the resurrection of Jesus, He talked to His disciples about their authority, which we see in Matthew 28:16–20:

> Then the eleven disciples went away into Galilee, to the mountain which Jesus had appointed for them. When they saw Him, they worshiped Him; but some doubted. And Jesus came and spoke to them, saying, "All authority has been given to Me in heaven and on earth. Go therefore and make disciples of all the nations, baptizing them in the name of the Father and of the Son and of the Holy Spirit, teaching them to observe all things that I have commanded you; and lo, I am with you always, even to the end of the age." Amen.

The Appointment

The story above does not talk about a nice farewell party that Jesus had with His disciples or some casual conversation He had near the end of His life with them. We are told in verse 16 that Jesus *made an appointment* with them to meet on the mountain. Remember that Jesus had spent every day with them for the last three-and-a-half years. But now He had something so important to communicate with them that He decided to make a specific appointment. It was like a preplanned audience with the Son of God. He obviously had something very important to say to them which He wanted to make sure they understood. If you study the Book of Acts, as well as church history, you will find out that they really understood what He taught them on that mountain.

Doing Things the Right Way Around

If we want to have the right results in anything we are doing, we have to do things the right way around. This might seem like commonsense to you, but I experience weekly that it is not so for many people. The Bible tells us that we must not worry about anything but release everything to God; then the peace of God will guard our minds and hearts.

Constantly, people ask me to pray for them for peace in their lives. Because I love people, I attempt to always be very honest with them. Before I say any prayer, I ask them if they worry about anything. Almost 100 percent of those people who lack peace worry about all sorts of things. I then tell them that my prayer for peace will bring no results in their lives. They are doing things the wrong way around. They tell me that they want God to give them peace—and then they will stop worrying. The right way around is to stop worrying, and then you will have peace.

We see this beautifully illustrated at this appointment which Jesus had with His disciples. Before Jesus told them *what* to do, in verse 19, He wanted to make sure that they understood *why* they needed to do it. In verse 18, He said to them, "All authority has been given to Me in heaven and on earth." Then He continued to tell them in verse 19, "Go therefore and make disciples of all the nations, baptizing them in the name of the Father and of the Son and of the Holy Spirit." Before He told them what to do, He informed them about their incredible authority which they now needed to walk in.

If we do don't learn to do things the right way around, the supernatural will be nothing but a theory—or possibly just a desire we have. In order to experience it and walk in it, we must do things the right way around. We can see this demonstrated in the very beginning of human history. When God created man, He did not just put him in the garden and tell him what to do. Let us look at what happened in Genesis 1:22:

> *And God blessed them, saying, "Be fruitful and multiply, and fill the waters in the seas, and let birds multiply on the earth."*

Before God told them what to do, He blessed them. This is the New Covenant. Everything starts with God and continues with our response to Him. God blessed them first, and then gave them instructions about what to do. Jesus told His disciples first what authority they had; then He told them what to do. The supernatural does not start with us or our desire to see the power of God. It starts with God. Therefore, I started this book showing you that it is God's desire more than ours to move in the supernatural. All we have to do is to respond to Him in the right way.

Power and Authority

In the original language of the New Testament, there are two main words which many languages translate as "power," yet these two words have different meanings depending on the context. The first word is *exousia,* and the second word is *dunamis.* While dunamis speaks of *actual power* as in a force, *exousia* speaks of *authoritative power,* also understood as legal right.[1]

In Matthew 28, when Jesus had the appointment with His disciples, He used the word *exousia,* which means "legal authority" rather than power. It is very important for Christians to understand that we have both—authority and power. If we only believe and walk in one of these two, we will not be able to walk in the supernatural as God has designed it for us.

Let me illustrate the difference of these two words in a simple way. A policeman has authority (*exousia*) to stop a car. When he stands in the middle of the road and puts out his hand, cars stop because they recognize his authority. The car actually has much more power (*dunamis*) than the policemen does and could easily run over the policeman and kill him. If the driver of the car happens to be a criminal, decides to ignore the authority of the policeman, and runs over him to kill him, then the authority of the policeman will not save him or stop the criminal. However, if the policemen uses his power (*dunamis*), which he can exercise through his gun, pulls it out, and points it at the forehead of the criminal, the criminal stands no chance. Authority alone is not enough. He needs authority and power.

If we truly want the supernatural to become a lifestyle for us, we have to walk in both—authority and power. Jesus has given us the highest authority that exists as well as the greatest power that exists. We are told in Acts 1:8,

> *But you shall receive power [dunamis] when the Holy Spirit has come upon you; and you shall be witnesses to Me in Jerusalem, and in all Judea and Samaria, and to the end of the earth.*

This is not talking about any human power. It is talking about the power of the Holy Spirit who is God Himself. I hope that through these next pages the Holy Spirit will inspire you and fill your heart with revelation of the incredible power and authority that belong to you. If your heart grasps this, you will learn to walk in the supernatural.

Endnote

1. *Exousia,* "authority," Strong's #1849; http://biblehub.com/greek/1849.htm, accessed 15 September 2016.

Testimony

My name is Hosanildo. I couldn't move my left arm for four months; I could not move it even as high as my head. I felt such a strong pain that it would not let me sleep or get dressed. For the glory of the Lord and for my happiness, a pastor was preaching in our church, in Diamantino, Brazil and he prophesied that from that moment on, I would never feel that pain again. In fact, I got healed, and now I can do my common activities and physical exercises.

Testimony

My name is Alexandro, I am from Frankfurt, Germany. After working in places that demanded a lot of effort, and also because of my weight, my knees were damaged. They seemed to get out of place, and my legs would tremble. I used to feel so much pain in my knees that I had to take anti-inflammatories, and I often had to wear bandages at work. I participated in a church service, and we were asked if anyone felt any pain in their body. On that day, my knees hurt a lot. After I received prayer, I was healed. Today, I do not feel as much pain as before, and I leave the bandages home. Actually, I do not use them anymore.

Chapter 16

Delegated Authority

Understanding the Bible

In order to correctly understand the Bible, we must remind ourselves that it was never written in chapters and verses. Those were added later by men who translated the Bible from the original so that we could more easily locate where something is written. If, in our reading of the Bible, we divide it into chapters and verses instead of understanding the whole context, we will miss important truths. When Jesus made that appointment with His disciples in order to communicate this important message, He did not say it in verses; He simply spoke. Let us look at Matthew 28:18–19 again in order to grasp what He truly said: *"All authority has been given to Me in heaven and on earth. Go therefore make disciples of all the nations."* One of the key words in this passage is the word *therefore* in verse nineteen. To paraphrase, Jesus said, "Listen guys, I have all the authority that anybody can have, and because of this, I also have the legal right to send anybody I want to in My authority. You are going because of My authority not because of your own cleverness, strength, or authority." The apostles clearly understood what Jesus was communicating, which is demonstrated throughout the whole Book of Acts. Why do we go and make disciples and reach the lost? We go because we have been commissioned by the highest authority in the universe. It is like Bill Gates, who is the richest man in the world, giving you his credit card and saying, "I have all the money in the world; go and do some business for me." It doesn't matter how poor you are, how weak or worthless you feel, or how limited your resources are. You would not be walking in your own authority, but in Bill Gates' authority.

Our authority does not come from screaming the name of Jesus at some demons. That will neither bother nor scare the devil. Our authority comes because it has been delegated to us by Jesus Himself, who has all authority in heaven and on earth. It is so important for us to understand this—not only so that we will walk in the confidence of this authority, but also so that we will understand that Jesus has delegated this to us and is now expecting for us to do His business here on earth.

In Matthew 8:5–11 and 13, we see a man who understood delegated authority:

Now when Jesus had entered Capernaum, a centurion came to Him, pleading with Him, saying, "Lord, my servant is lying at home paralyzed, dreadfully tormented." And Jesus said to him, "I will come and heal him." The centurion answered and said, "Lord, I am not worthy that You should come under my roof. But only speak a word, and my servant will be healed. For I also am a man under authority, having soldiers under me. And I say to this one, 'Go,' and he goes; and to another, 'Come,' and he comes; and to my servant, 'Do this,' and he does it." When Jesus heard it, He marveled, and said to those who followed, "Assuredly, I say to you, I have not found such great faith, not even in Israel! And I say to you that many will come from east and west, and sit down with Abraham, Isaac, and Jacob in the kingdom of heaven. "But the sons of the kingdom will be cast out into outer darkness. There will be weeping and gnashing of teeth." Then Jesus said to the centurion, "Go your way; and as

you have believed, so let it be done for you."
And his servant was healed that same hour

This man asked Jesus to heal his servant, and Jesus was willing to do so. The centurion said that Jesus didn't need to go with him; He had only to speak, and the servant would be healed. The centurion had such incredible faith because he understood delegated authority. Jesus responded that He had never seen such great faith. This very interesting statement tells us that the greatest faith is the one that understands and believes in delegated authority. Unless we understand, believe, and walk in delegated authority, the supernatural will not be a regular part of our lives.

Look at what the centurion said to Jesus in verse 9: *"For I also am a man under authority having soldiers under me. I say to this one 'Go' and he goes; to another one 'Come' and he comes; and to my servant, 'Do this' and he does it."* He fully understood that his authority over his servant was not of himself but was delegated to him. He was under the authority of the Roman Empire, which was the most powerful empire of the time. When he said anything to his servants, he understood it was as if the Roman emperor Caesar himself was speaking. Nobody could resist Caesar's authority without suffering serious consequences. Because the centurion understood and believed in this delegated authority, he knew that all Jesus had to do was speak and heaven would respond. Jesus did not walk in His own authority; He walked in the authority of God the Creator of the universe. Jesus sent us to preach the gospel and do the same works that He did and even greater ones; therefore, our authority is equal to His.

An important principle about moving in this level of authority is to understand that it has been delegated to us. Sadly, I have witnessed people who began to believe in their authority in Christ, exercised it, and then fell in pride and the temptation of the devil to make them believe that they were someone special. Eventually, they thought that the authority they were walking in was their own authority. That always ended in a lot of pain for themselves and others who were involved. The only way to be safe and walk in this authority of heaven is to be under the authority of heaven.

The apostle James tells us this as well: "Therefore submit to God. Resist the devil and he will flee from you" (James 4:7). I have heard this scripture quoted out of context many times. People have told me, *"Resist the devil, and he will flee from you."* I do not believe that is the whole truth. It is only part of the truth. We are told to submit to God first, and then to resist the devil. Why is this so important? It is so important because our authority is not in ourselves; it is delegated to us from God. Since we are not the source of the authority, we must submit to the higher authority who delegated it to us in the first place so that we can have and walk in this authority.

Let me give you an example: if you run your business contrary to the Word of God and the devil attacks your business, you have no authority to resist him because you rebelled against the one who delegated authority over the devil to you. In every area of our lives, we must understand that we are never the source of our authority. Since this authority has been delegated to us by God, we can only use it within the framework which He outlined in His Word. We cannot do with it whatever we desire; we must exercise it in submission to God who delegated it to us.

If we truly understand this simple truth and are surrendered and submitted to Christ who delegated His authority to us, then we can exercise that same authority. If you are interested in finding out more about the importance of obedience, I wrote a chapter about it in my book *Radical*. Obedience is something that should be normal in the life of every Christian.

No Limit

Is there any limit to the authority that we have been given? That is a very important question that we have to answer. Let us turn to the discourse that Jesus gave His disciples at the appointment on the mountain. In Matthew 28:18, Jesus told them, "All authority has been given to Me *in heaven and on earth.*" The word *all* simply means "all," which means *there is no limit.* Jesus told His disciples that there is absolutely no limit to His authority. He told them that He had all authority in heaven *and* on earth, which means that He has more authority than the presidents of the United States, Brazil, or any other nation of the world.

Most Christians would agree with me on this issue. However, do you remember that Jesus said that His disciples were sent *because* He has all authority? When He said, "Therefore go," He linked the commandment to go directly to His authority which He delegated to them. We, as the disciples of Jesus Christ, have the same authority that He Himself does.

Dream with me, my friend, and imagine that all over the world Christians begin to understand and believe in the authority that they have been given by Christ, which is without limit. If that happened, we would change the world. It is time to stop criticizing and complaining about the state that our countries are in; instead, let us use our limitless authority to change nations.

Jesus illustrated this in another statement which He made in John 20:21: *"So Jesus said to them again, 'Peace to you! As the Father has sent Me, I also send you.'"* The meaning in the original here is very clear. It means that *in exactly the same way* the Father sent Jesus, Jesus sent us. When the Father sent Jesus, He delegated His authority to Him. Jesus sent us *in exactly the same way* and delegated His authority to us. My friend, submit to Christ's authority and exercise His limitless authority everywhere you go. When I pray for the sick, in my mind's eye I imagine Jesus speaking to the sickness and commanding it to go—because when I pray, it is in His authority, so it is exactly as if He was doing it.

Testimony

My name is Beate, I am from Berlin, Germany. Because of a constant pain in my abdomen, I went to the doctor. She examined me and performed an ultrasound through which they found a 4 cm lump on my left kidney. But, according to her, that was not where all the pain came from. To check further, she asked for some blood exams and an MRI. The following Sunday, at the end of the church service, I went to the front to receive some prayer. I told a sister from church about the pain in my abdomen and the possible lump. We prayed for peace and rest from God and for the lump to leave my body in the name of Jesus. The appointment for the MRI would take a while, so the doctor asked me to do a computer tomography. My family, my cell group, and many people from church prayed for me; it is so amazing how I started to feel peace. With time, all abdominal pain disappeared. They did the tomography throughout my abdominal area up to my lungs, with and without the contrast product. When I received the diagnosis, the result was *orthotropic kidney, normal size. Normal adrenals.* (There was no lump in my kidneys.) No more exams were needed. I am so thankful to the Lord because He healed me. I experienced His peace filling me so that there was no place for anxiety or fear.

Testimony

My name is Ozanir, and I am from Diamantina, Brazil. For more than four months, I could not raise my left arm. I could not sleep well or wear a t-shirt. At a church meeting, I received a word from God. He said that from that moment on, I would be free from every pain in my left arm. I was immediately healed, and I have never felt that pain again.

Chapter 17

Our Legal Rights

We said in a previous chapter that *exousia,* the Greek word for *authority,* means "legal power" or "legal right." What legal rights do we have? That is a very important question. The apostle Paul tells us in 2 Corinthians 5:20, *"Now then, we are ambassadors for Christ, as though God were pleading through us: we implore you on Christ's behalf, be reconciled to God."*

What is an ambassador? An ambassador is somebody who represents the authority of his or her own country. An ambassador has the legal right to exercise that authority wherever he or she has been sent. We are ambassadors for Christ, which means that we live, walk, and speak with precisely the same authority that Christ does. We will only experience this if our theology in this area is that of Arminius, which is *dynamic*—and not that of Calvin, which is *determined.* We could have all the authority in the universe and not walk in it.

There is an Australian man named Julian Assange who is the founder of WikiLeaks, an internet platform that published secret information from governments all over the world. Because Assange leaked top-secret information, the Americans wanted to arrest him and put him on trial, which could have resulted in a death sentence for him. He was in London and fled into the Ecuadorian Embassy.

The Americans did everything they could to get him expedited to the United States, putting a lot of pressure on the British government. Day and night, the British government posted special police forces outside the door of the Ecuadorian Embassy. They really wanted to arrest Julian Assange, but they had to wait for him to leave the embassy of his own free will. They cannot enter that embassy.

The Ecuadorian Embassy is right in the middle of London, yet for years Julian has remained untouchable for the British government. They cannot not touch him even though he has been in their own country—simply because the Ecuadorian Embassy allowed him to stay with them. The British government has absolutely no authority to enter that building. If they had entered the embassy, it would be as if they had attacked Ecuador and declared war.

This picture beautifully demonstrates the authority that we have in Christ. We are ambassadors for Jesus Christ who live in this world, yet we are completely untouchable for the devil, the ruler of this world. As long as we understand and believe in our authority and remain under the authority of Christ, we are His ambassadors who exercise His authority.

How Far Does It Reach?

Our authority is not limited to a certain place. Jesus told His disciples in Matthew 28:18, "All authority has been given to Me *in heaven and on earth.*" The authority of Jesus reaches all of heaven and all of earth. It is my personal conviction that the world is in such a terrible state partially because the sons and daughters of God do not exercise Christ's authority. Jesus taught us to pray for the kingdom of God to come and for His will to be done on earth as it is in heaven. In heaven, there is no questioning of God's authority. Any command He gives to any of the angels is absolutely obeyed without any discussion. God desires greatly that His will be done on earth in the same way. If

Chrisitians all over the world rise up to this desire of the heart of God and exercise His authority on earth, then His will shall be done here as it is in heaven.

We have to be convinced about God's will in heaven in order to see it manifest here on earth. There is no sickness or disease in heaven, and there is neither poverty nor sin. There is no hatred, anger, or disunity; there is only love. God desires for us to exercise our authority and make earth a better place.

When Jesus sent His disciples out to preach in Matthew 10:7–8, He told them,

> *And as you go, preach, saying, "The kingdom of heaven is at hand." Heal the sick, cleanse the lepers, raise the dead, cast out demons. Freely you have received, freely give.*

Jesus not only told His disciples to preach the gospel, but He also told them specifically to say, "The kingdom of heaven is at hand." In chapter 4, we saw that the kingdom equals power. Jesus told them to demonstrate the authority of His kingdom. He does not want us to only talk about His love; He wants us to demonstrate it with signs, wonders, and miracles. The commission of Jesus was very clear: preach, heal the sick, cleanse the lepers, raise the dead, cast out demons, and don't charge for it. They moved in such incredible authority because they received it from Him. When He told them that they freely received it, He wanted them to understand that they were not the source of their authority.

What Are Our Legal Rights?

Whatever our legal right is, it is God's offer—but not neccessarily our guarantee. There are countless kings and priests (Rev. 1:6) of God who live like beggars simply because they do not believe Him and claim their legal rights. We do not have time to go through all of our legal rights in this book, but I will show you some of them.

The first legal right that we have is to be sons of God. As we see in John 1:12, *"But as many as received him, to them gave he power [exousia] to become the sons of God, even to them that believe on his name"* (KJV). The word in the original for *power* is the Greek word *exousia*, which we have seen means "a legal right." Everybody who has received Christ has the *legal right* to be God's own son or daughter. As such, and by faith, we have access to everything that belongs to Him.

The second legal right we have is the right to inherit. Romans 8:15–17 tells us,

> *For you did not receive the spirit of bondage again to fear, but you received the Spirit of adoption by whom we cry out, "Abba, Father." The Spirit Himself bears witness with our spirit that we are children of God, and if children, then heirs—heirs of God and joint heirs with Christ, if indeed we suffer with Him, that we may also be glorified together*

Since we have the legal right to be children, as we just saw earlier, we also now have the legal right of inheritance. The wonderful thing is that we have become joint heirs with Jesus Himself. To be a *joint heir* means that *everything that belongs to Him also belongs to me*. This is one of the most powerful truths of the New Covenant, which I plan to write about in my next book; therefore, I won't go into much detail here.

The third legal right that we have is to have our prayers answered. We are told in John 14:13–14, *"And whatever you ask in My name, that I will do, that the Father may be glorified in the Son. "If you ask anything in My name, I will do it."* There is not one word in the Bible that is written by chance or wasted. Here Jesus repeats Himself in order to emphasize this truth of our legal right. He told us that we can ask anything in His name and He will do it for us.

If we want to experience this legal right of answered prayer, we must understand what it means to pray "in His name." It certainly does not mean to add the phrase "in the name of Jesus" at the end of our prayers. There is nothing wrong with doing this, unless it is done as a religious habit without true faith in our legal right. We do not have this legal right because we say "in the name of Jesus," but because we understand our authority in Christ. As New Covenant believers who desire to see the supernatural power of heaven, we have to stop begging God and begin to demand our legal right.

When I come to God in prayer, I am aware that I am in Christ; therefore, what I demand from

Him is just the same as if Jesus Himself were demanding something. God would not turn down Jesus; therefore, He will not turn down my request either. Unless our thinking and believing changes in this area, the supernatural will not be a daily part of our lives. I daily meet Christians who say or pray something adding the words, "In the name of Jesus," hoping it will be theirs. They are not convinced that it already belongs to them. Jesus emphasized this truth in the very next chapter; in John 15:7, He said, *"If you abide in Me, and My words abide in you, you will ask what you desire, and it shall be done for you."*

The fourth legal right that we have is authority over all the works of the devil. The apostle Paul understood this truth so well and taught it to us so beautifully in the epistle to the Ephesians.

> *. . . and raised us up together, and made us sit together in the heavenly places in Christ Jesus. . . .*
>
> —EPHESIANS 2:6

> *. . . which He worked in Christ when He raised Him from the dead and seated Him at His right hand in the heavenly places, far above all principality and power and might*

and dominion, and every name that is named, not only in this age but also in that which is to come. And He put all things under His feet . . .

—EPHESIANS 1:20–22

Since our authority is in Christ, we have the same authority that He has over all demonic power, which the Scriptures clearly demonstrate. Christ is seated in the heavenly places over absolutely every power, might, and dominion. We are seated with Him; therefore, every power, might, and dominion is also under our feet. We are told in 1 John 3:8, *"For this purpose the Son of God was manifested, that He might destroy the works of the devil."*

Since we walk and live in His authority, we are also called to destroy the works of the devil. We have to use our God-given authority over the works of the devil which include sickness, disease, brokenness, and addictions. It is utterly our responsibility to exercise this authority as we are told in Psalm 115:16: "The heaven, even the heavens, are the LORD's; but the earth He has given to the children of men." Since God has given us authority over this earth, we have to use it in order to establish His kingdom. We have to learn to declare, demand, and decree—and in doing so, use our God-given authority.

Testimony

My name is Socorro, I mam from Brasilia, Brazil. I had cataracts for five years, and all the exams indicated I was ready for surgery. But then I participated in a conference, and I was healed that night. After repeating all the exams, it was proved that I was healed. Thank You, Lord, because I know You healed me.

Testimony

My name is Joanilda. I had very strong pain close to my kidneys for many days. I went to the doctor because I couldn't bear it anymore. Even before doing any exams, I asked a brother in church to pray for me for healing. When I told him about the pain, I told him one of my kidneys was stunted, like a deflated balloon and its functions were limited. Then, I received some prayer for the pain and for the restoration of my kidney. After some new exams, I found out two important things: Firstly, the pain was not from my kidney but from my back; and secondly, the sick kidney had been restored, and it was working perfectly. Glory to God.

Chapter 18

How to Walk in Our Authority

Hindrances to Walking in Authority

If we truly desire to walk in our God-given authority, we must recognize that there are things that hinder us from walking in that authority. We have to be absolutely ruthless and hate everything that hinders us from walking in our authority.

Many years ago, Jesus appeared to me in a prophetic dream that impacted my life very deeply. For many months after that dream, I was greatly disturbed and cried many tears over the sad truth that Jesus showed me in the dream. With the saddest look in His eyes and the strongest emotion of sadness imaginable, He told me that 90 percent of all God's children are just children, and only 10 percent are true disciples.

As I began to pray and think about what He said, I realized how few Christians really walk in their authority. I have always been passionate to teach, preach, and motivate people to follow Christ radically. After that dream, however, my passion for the truth about our authority was not only confirmed, but also increased. I determined all the more to not only be one of the 10 percent but to change that number for the glory of our King.

Just a few weeks ago, I heard a statistic that only 10 percent of all people apply the knowledge that they already have. It is not what you know about your legal authority that will cause you to live in it; it is how much of it you apply to your life. With all of my heart, I pray and believe that God will use this book to change that number. Following are some main hindrances that will stop us from walking in our God-given authority.

Unbelief is the first thing that will hinder us. Unbelief is a terrible thing that must be rejected with all of our strength. There is a big difference between unbelief and doubt, which I will explain to you in the next point. An unbelieving person will never be able to walk in their God-given authority. To believe that God *can* heal you is not biblical faith that brings miracles into our lives. Often, as I travel and pray for people who are sick, I ask them this question: *"Do you believe that God will heal you right now?"* The majority of them answer, *"Yes, pastor, I do believe with all of my heart that God can heal me.*" If there is a God who created the universe, then He certainly has to be able to heal; otherwise, He would not be God. True faith always believes that God *does* what He says, not just that God *can do* what He says.

The second hindrance is *doubt*. A powerful prophet in America recently had a powerful dream. In that dream, he saw a small white cloud, and the Lord told him to warn His people about this dangerous, raging cloud. The man was shocked by the alarm in the voice of Jesus and wanted to know how such a small, white cloud could be so dangerous. Jesus replied that this cloud has the potential to steal every spiritual blessing from the people of God. Our authority in Christ is one of these spiritual blessings. As the prophet inquired in the dream, *"What is this cloud?"* The Lord answered him, *"It is the cloud of doubt."* He immediately understood how dangerous that cloud was. James warns us about this danger:

> *But let him ask in faith, with no doubting, for he who doubts is like a wave of the sea driven and tossed by the wind. For let not that man suppose that he will receive*

anything from the Lord; he is a double-minded man, unstable in all his ways.
—JAMES 1:6–8

Two things strike me in this passage. First of all, a person who doubts will not receive anything from the Lord, and second, that person is unstable in all his ways. We are told that we have to ask with no doubt, which is a very strong statement. You can have 99.9 percent faith and 0.1 percent doubt, which would already disqualify you from receiving anything from the Lord. We are *not* told that God will not give anything to this person; we are told that this person will not *receive* anything. It is not God who withholds anything from the doubter; it is the doubter who cannot get hold of it.

The word *receive* is a strong word in the original which means "to lay hold of with your hands and seize it." Jesus told us that we must have faith without doubt. God has put His faith into our hearts; doubt is a choice that we make. God is a good God, who will not withhold things from the doubter, but the doubter will not live in his spiritual authority because he will not get hold of it.

What then is this difference between unbelief and doubt? Unbelief does not believe that

God either will do or has done what He said. Doubt wavers. It is like a wave tossed by the wind and the sea. Imagine you are in a meeting with a strong anointing or are reading this book and feel inspired. You decide to believe for supernatural provision. You boldly declare and tell your friends that God is your provider.

Tomorrow morning when you drive to work, your car breaks down, and you do not have the money to repair it. When you come home from work in the evening, you find an unexpected bill in your mail. Suddenly, you begin to waver because your circumstances have changed. Instead of focusing on what you heard in the meeting or read in this book, you now put your focus on your circumstances and so open your heart to doubt. You call your leader and pour out your heart of frustration and desperation. Your leader prays with you and encourages you to believe God to be your provider. You make a decision to believe again that God will take care of all your problems, and then you feel better.

The next day you lose your job. Now you are frustrated again and begin to doubt that God will provide for you. While unbelief does not believe that God will do what He said, doubt changes its belief depending on the feelings or circumstances. If you want to walk in the supernatural, you must daily renounce all doubt from your life.

The third thing that hinders us is *relying on our feelings*. Our feelings are very subjective, which means that they are not reliable, and they lie to us. If I were to ask you the question, "Have you ever been in a meeting where you felt the strong presence of God?" I am sure you would answer, "Yes." If I then asked you if you had ever been in a meeting where you felt oppression and no presence of God at all, you would most likely answer yes to that question also. I thank God that early in my ministry I learned this secret: I will not let my feelings determine what I believe. How subjective our feelings are is shown by the answers to the above two questions. The truth is that God is omnipresent and was in both of those meetings, looking for channels through whom He could exercise His authority.

Recently, I was preaching for three nights in a church that had a lot of problems. I felt no presence of God and much oppression. I remember well that, as I was preaching, strong thoughts came to my mind that no miracles would happen that night and no prophecies would be released. In that instant, I made a decision to not let those thoughts and feelings influence what I believe and how I would act. I deliberately told the church that I would pray for every sick person in the meeting. My feelings told me that was a stupid thing to do and that I would regret it. In that very meeting—where I felt like leaving immediately after I was finished preaching, but chose instead not to follow my feelings—Jesus did many outstanding miracles, including opening a deaf ear, visibly removing a tumor, and restoring the eyesight of a girl who could not see without her thick glasses.

The fourth hindrance is *trying to copy a technique.* Many men and women of God walk in their authority because they understand and believe the principle of authority and who they are in Christ. Unfortunately, many people want to copy them and think the supernatural can be obtained through a technique. I remember the time well, very recently, when a couple came to me in Europe, impressed by what they saw God do through me and asked me to impart the same to them too by laying hands on them and praying for them. I told them that the fruit of my ministry and the authority I walk in does not come from a technique or because somebody laid hands on me. It is a result of my choice to follow Christ relentlessly and pursue the supernatural through radical commitment to prayer, studying the Bible, and fasting. I do believe in the laying on of hands, but I do not believe that you will get what I have if I were to lay hands on you. You can only get it from the source, who is the Lord. I am very determined never to make disciples of Reinhard, only disciples of Jesus Christ.

How to Walk in Our Authority

If we want to walk practically in the supernatural, we have to understand some important principles. If you apply these truths in your life, I am convinced that you will also experience the supernatural in your life:

> *Spending time with Jesus.* We are not called to a religion; we are called to a relationship. Christ in us is the hope of glory (Col. 1:27). Since it is His authority that we walk in, I think it would be pretty smart to walk close to Him.

Nothing will substitute for
your relationship with Jesus.
Become a friend of the Holy Spirit. I do
not want to talk much about
this as I already talked about
it in greater detail in a
previous chapter. It is the
Holy Spirit who teaches us all
things, helps us to apply the
knowledge of the Bible, and
enables us practically to live a
supernatural lifestyle.
Learn to live a life of faith. Again, I
don't want to spend time
teaching you about the life of
faith here. I have written a
whole book all about that
subject. If you need to know
more about faith, then I
recommend that you get my
book, which is simply called
Faith. You have to understand
that nobody can walk in their
God-given authority, unless
they do so by faith.
Spend time studying the Bible. It never
ceases to amaze me, even

after so many years in the ministry, how little time Christians spend studying the Bible. It is the Word of God that transforms our hearts and lives and teaches us to live in the supernatural. In my book *Radical,* I teach how we can learn to meditate and benefit from the Word of God.

Be disciplined. It is the disciplined that take the world, walk in their authority, and live a supernatural lifestyle. I personally do not know anybody who has been fruitful in their ministry or achieved something significant without being disciplined. Discipline yourself. Go to bed earlier, get out of bed earlier, spend time in the presence of Jesus, and the supernatural will become part of your life. One of my spiritual fathers was a man who trained Dr. Yonggi Cho, the pastor of the largest church in the world, for the ministry. That man was extremely disciplined and constantly told me how extremely disciplined Dr. Yonggi Cho was too. Dr. Cho would never allow anyone or anything to stop him from getting up early and spending time with God. Part of the fruit of the Spirit is self-discipline.

I deeply desire to see a church where every member walks in the supernatural. This desire is not motivated by the longing for power, but by a heart that longs for Christ to be glorified. Before Jesus returns, His body will move in the supernatural, beyond what the Book of Acts experienced. The Book of Acts does not end properly; it stops abruptly because God is not yet finished writing it. May He continue writing it through you and me.

Testimony

My name is Maria Helena, and I live in Guaratuba, Brazil. Yesterday at the church meeting, I was invited to receive prayer because I have had problems with my knees. I had arthrosis for two years. I could not walk; I cried a lot. People had to pick me up at home to bring me to church services. After I received prayer, I noticed I was healed, but I did not say anything about it. I thought, "I will go home and check it. I do not want to give a false testimony." But today I was able to work normally. I came to church service by bicycle. I could walk all day long for the honor and the glory of Jesus. I am healed. Everything is normal.

Testimony

My name is Cecília, and I am 50. I live in Guaratuba, Brazil. I used to have many cysts in my breasts, especially in the right breast. I've been fighting cysts in one of my breasts for nine years. I've already done biopsies, punctures, and other kinds of exams. Yesterday, when I received prayer, God did a miracle in my life. During the prayer time, I felt I was being healed. I felt those nodes being taken away. Some minutes later, I touched my breasts, and the nodes were truly gone. For the honor and glory of the Lord, I was healed.

Chapter 19

God Loves to Heal

Divine healing is a very big subject, which we cannot study in detail here. We would need to write an entire book if we wanted to truly study this subject in depth. I have decided to dedicate one chapter to this subject to stir and challenge your thinking.

The Important Question

Does God always want to heal everybody? This is a very important question that many people are not sure how to answer. They believe that God *can* heal, but are not convinced that God always *wants* to or *will* heal. This question is very important for us to settle in our hearts since only by faith can we receive our healing miracle. Without an assurance of the will of God, there is no biblical faith. We must base what we believe on the Word of God and not the opinion of man.

In Matthew 8:14–17, we read a beautiful account of Jesus healing all the sick that came to Him:

Now when Jesus had come into Peter's house, He saw his wife's mother lying sick with a fever. So He touched her hand, and the fever left her. And she arose and served them. When evening had come, they brought to Him many who were demon-possessed. And He cast out the spirits with a word, and healed all who were sick, that it might be fulfilled which was spoken by Isaiah the prophet, saying: "He Himself took our infirmities and bore our sicknesses."

Why did Jesus heal all the sick that came to Him in this account? He did so because He loved them and cared for them, but *also* in order to fulfill the Word of God. Verse 17 tells us "that it might be fulfilled which was spoken by Isaiah the prophet, saying: 'He Himself took our infirmities and bore our sicknesses.'" It is very important to notice that Jesus healed all those who came to Him in order to fulfill the promise spoken by the prophet Isaiah:

Surely He has borne our griefs and carried our sorrows; yet we esteemed Him stricken, smitten by God, and afflicted. But He was wounded for our transgressions, He was bruised for our iniquities; the chastisement for our peace was upon Him, and by His stripes we are healed.

—Isaiah 53:4–5

The same scripture that promises us that Jesus took all of our sins also promises that He heals all of our diseases. God not only wanted to tell the people through the prophet Isaiah that He would send His Son Jesus to die for their sins and sicknesses, but He also wanted it demonstrated through the life of Christ. We are told in Psalm 103:2–3, *"Bless the LORD, O my soul, and forget not all His benefits: who forgives all your iniquities, who heals all your diseases."* Once again, the same scripture that promises us forgiveness, promises us healings. How many sins are we promised to be forgiven? All of them! And how many diseases are we promised to be healed of? All of them!

After studying this subject of divine healing for most of my Christian life, I have arrived at two conclusions: First, God always wants His children to be healed; and second, regarding this subject, there will be questions that we will not have answered until we are in heaven. Many times I have been asked, "If God wants to heal everybody, then why is everybody not healed?" I like to answer this question by asking another question, "If God wants everybody to be saved, then why is everybody not saved?"

God's Heart

Acts 10:38 is a scripture that I particularly love because it expresses the heart of God so beautifully:

> . . . *how God anointed Jesus of Nazareth with the Holy Spirit and with power, who went about doing good and healing all who were oppressed by the devil, for God was with Him.*

The reason why this expresses the heart of God so beautifully is because we see the Trinity united in purpose. God the Father desired to heal the people, His Son Jesus was the perfect channel, and the third part of the Godhead, the Holy Spirit, enabled Him to do so. God not only *can* heal you; He *wants* to heal you—as we see in Mark 1:40–41:

> *Now a leper came to Him, imploring Him, kneeling down to Him and saying to Him, "If You are willing, You can make me clean." Then Jesus, moved with compassion,*

stretched out His hand and touched him and said to him, "I am willing; be cleansed."

Jesus has compassion and wants to heal you as He demonstrated in this scripture. Just as salvation has to be received by faith, so healing can only be received by faith. God often will use people as channels to bring His healing power to His children. This is wonderful and dangerous at the same time. If you put your trust in the channel rather than the source of the healing—which is God and the finished work of the cross—you will most likely end up disappointed. Your faith has to be in God and in God alone.

As you study the Gospels, you will see that Jesus healed in various ways. I believe that expresses His determination to heal people. Many times, I have asked myself the question, "Why did Jesus heal people in so many different ways?" There are at least two reasons why He did so. Firstly, He wanted to show us that we must not follow a technique, but put our trust in Jesus alone. Secondly, He wanted to teach us that we have to receive our healing by faith. In the following scriptures, you will see these two truths emphasized. He healed in many different ways, and people needed to receive their healing by faith.

> *Then Jesus said to the centurion, "Go your way; and as you have believed, so let it be done for you." And his servant was healed that same hour.*
>
> —MATTHEW 8:13

> *Then Jesus answered and said to her, "O woman, great is your faith! Let it be to you as you desire." And her daughter was healed from that very hour.*
>
> —MATTHEW 15:28

> *Now a certain woman had a flow of blood for twelve years, and had suffered many things from many physicians. She had spent all that she had and was no better, but rather grew worse. When she heard about Jesus, she came behind Him in the crowd and touched His garment. For she said, "If only I may touch His clothes, I shall be made well." Immediately the fountain of her blood was dried up, and she felt in her body that she was healed of the affliction.*
>
> —MARK 5:25–29

> *Now as Jesus passed by, He saw a man who was blind from birth. And His*

disciples asked Him, saying, "Rabbi, who sinned, this man or his parents, that he was born blind?" Jesus answered, "Neither this man nor his parents sinned, but that the works of God should be revealed in him. I must work the works of Him who sent Me while it is day; the night is coming when no one can work. As long as I am in the world, I am the light of the world." When He had said these things, He spat on the ground and made clay with the saliva; and He anointed the eyes of the blind man with the clay. And He said to him, "Go, wash in the pool of Siloam" (which is translated, Sent). So he went and washed, and came back seeing.

—JOHN 9:1–7

Then as He entered a certain village, there met Him ten men who were lepers, who stood afar off. And they lifted up their voices and said, "Jesus, Master, have mercy on us!" So when He saw them, He said to them, "Go, show yourselves to the priests." And so it was that as they went, they were cleansed.

—LUKE 17:12–14

There are, of course, exceptions when God heals people without their own faith being involved. In *some* cases, God can release gifts of faith, healings, and miracles that are independent from the faith of the people who receive the miracle. I remember when I preached in a large church and God told me that He would heal a woman in the meeting who had a broken shoulder. The lady came to the front and was unable to move her shoulder because of the fracture. She did not believe that she would get a miracle, but because God gave me a word of knowledge, a gift of faith, and a gift of miracle, it made no difference to me what that lady believed. I knew she would get healed, and she did. Our faith must not be in our faith, but in the finished work of the cross of Jesus Christ.

Testimony

My name is Mira, and I am from Curitiba, Brazil. I was at the church building, leaving for an *Encounter with God* weekend. They had recently put a glass door there, and as I was walking through this door, someone called my name. As I turned to see who it was, I hit my face on the door. I immediately felt great pain. My husband and my son were going to serve at that encounter. I went back home, put some ice on my nose, and went to bed. It was really hard to sleep that night because of the pain. When I woke up, I noticed that my eyes were black. It hurt so much I could barely touch my nose with my hand. I did not go to the hospital immediately because I already had an appointment with the doctor on Wednesday because of a headache and rhinitis. The following Wednesday I went to the doctor and had some exams. The doctor found out my nose was broken. I went to another hospital, and the doctor told me I had to have plastic surgery, a nose job, immediately. I talked to my doctor (an otolaryngologist), and he confirmed the fracture and the need for surgery. I started the process to undergo surgery the following Friday.

The day before the surgery, there was a preacher at our church, and, as I sat in the front row to listen to him, I observed that he had opened a bottle of water and started to drink it. As he finished preaching, he threw that water on people while he prayed. He shouted, "I release the healing power of Jesus." Because I was in the front row, I received a great amount of the water straight in my face. It hurt a lot because my nose was broken. After that, the pastor started praying for all the people in church. The following morning, I went to the hospital. When I got there, the doctor examined my nose and asked for another X-ray exam. He wanted to see exactly where the procedure needed to take place. As he looked at the results, he found it strange because there was nothing broken. He showed me the exams and told me he could not operate on me because there was no evidence of a fracture. That's when I remembered what happened, and I started laughing. I told him a man of God threw water on the people, and that when the water hit my face, I was healed and freed from the need for surgery. Glory to God!

Chapter 20

Hindrances to Receiving Your Healing

By no means do I believe that I have all the answers regarding why some people are not healed. There can be numerous reasons, and only God alone knows for sure. We must never judge anyone or assume we know why some people are not healed, unless the Holy Spirit reveals it to us without the shadow of a doubt. We must always remember that walking in love, not walking in the supernatural *per se*, is our highest goal. But some hindrances are pretty clear, and I will talk about these here. Some of these hindrances are the same as I have mentioned in the chapter on authority; therefore, I will not go into much detail here.

Unbelief and doubt are two of our greatest enemies for not receiving our healings. In Mark 6:5–6, we find a very sad statement regarding unbelief connected to divine healing: *"Now He could do no mighty work there except that He laid His hands on a few sick people and He healed them. And He marveled because of their unbelief."*

Another great hindrance is to believe that we are not worthy to be healed. This is Old Covenant thinking that is based on a religion of works, and this must be removed from our thinking. We have been made worthy through the finished work of the cross alone.

Not removing the causes of the sicknesses from our lives can also be a reason for not receiving our healing. I want to make it very clear that I dare not believe or say that every unhealed sickness has sin as its cause. However, sin *can* be a reason why some people have not received their healing. We do not need to dig around in our subconscious for some previous sin that may have caused our sickness; we simply need to ask the Holy Spirit and let Him show us if there is something there or not.

I was preaching in a church in Europe and praying for the sick after the meeting. A lady came forward who had stomach ulcers, terrible pain in her back, and a shoulder that she could not use properly. As I laid my hands on her and began to pray, the Holy Spirit told me that she was sick because her heart was full of unforgiveness toward her brother. I told the Lord quietly in my heart that

I did not want to tell her that because I did not want to pass on a judgment. But the Holy Spirit, in His kindness, helped me and said, "Tell her what I told you, and that, as a sign of my love and desire to heal her, I will instantly heal her shoulder. But then she must forgive her brother if she wants to be completely healed."

As I told her what the Holy Spirit had told me and prayed for her shoulder, she was instantly healed and pain-free. I asked her if she was willing to forgive her brother, which she affirmed with tears. She pulled out her phone and crying she said, "I have not spoken to him in sixteen years because I am so angry at him." She forgave him, reconciled with him, and was completely healed. Even though sin can be a reason for the sickness, God still desires to heal us. The cross has dealt with sin and sickness together.

If you believe that God will make His children sick in order to teach them something, then you should never go to the doctor to find release from your suffering, as that would be rebellion against the will of God. I am absolutely not against doctors and medication, but I am against people saying that God sent their sickness and then going to the doctor to have it removed. That is hypocrisy.

Removing the Roots and Not the Fruits

The American Medical Society established that about fifty percent of all sicknesses are not of physical origin. It has been scientifically proven that our immune system, if it is healthy and functioning the way it was designed by God to function, will destroy every sickness and disease, even the most aggressive cancer cells. The number one factor that weakens and even shuts down the human immune system is stress. I do not believe that stress is caused by circumstances, but by our unbelieving reaction toward our circumstances. If our response to all circumstances is a response of faith, and if we follow sound biblical advice about how to live our lives, we will not be stressed.

Almost 30 years ago when we planted our first church, there was a healing evangelist from England who came to another city about an hour from where we lived. We organized for our whole church, which was only about 70 people at that time, to go to that meeting. The evangelist moved incredibly in the word of knowledge and healing, and we wanted our members to experience that. We had one lady of about 65 years of age in our church who desperately needed a miracle. She had suddenly developed an inflamation in her shoulder which caused her much pain and left her unable to use that shoulder. She went to many doctors and specialists, but nobody could help her. Many times we prayed for her without any result.

When the evangelist began to minister, there were about 200 people in the meeting, all unknown to him. One of the first words of knowledge he had described exactly and in great detail the lady from our church. He described things like her age, some other very specific details about her life, and the sickness so exactly that it could only have been God. It could only have been her, and she was the only one who responded. As her pastor, I got so excited for her because I had suffered with her (emotionally speaking) for several months already. As she went to the front, God said to me, "Watch closely because I am teaching you a very important lesson. I want you to learn to remove roots and not just cut off the bad fruit."

I was watching very closely, having no idea what was about to happen. As the evangelist prayed for her, she was immediately and forcefully knocked to the ground under the power of God and laid there for a while. I was even more excited then, seeing the great power of God and expecting her to finally receive her miracle. The evangelist ministered to some other people while she laid on the floor. When she finally got up, she was *not healed*. Everybody, including me, was confused and puzzled. Then God said to me; "The root of her sickness is resentment toward her sister who has cheated her out of an inheritance." We had all been trying to remove the bad *fruit* instead of cutting off the bad *root*.

During the rest of the meeting, as well as on the drive home, I was thinking about that experience. I talked to Debi and told her that I did not want to tell this nice lady and prominent member of our church that she had resentment and unforgiveness in her heart. Debi encouraged me that, as her pastor and out of love, I must talk to her. So after prayer, I decided to talk in a very loving way to her. I was hoping for her to be thankful, to then let go of her resentment, and to be healed. Unfortunately, she got very angry and eventually even left our church.

Body, Soul, and Spirit

We are told in 3 John 2, *"Beloved, I pray that you may prosper in all things and be in health, just as your soul prospers."* The apostle John makes a connection between physical health and the well-being of our soul. For centuries, people thought that sickness only had a physical origin. However, it is becoming clearer and clearer these days, because of scientific evidence, that people's mental and emotional attitudes frequently determine the physical health of that person.

We cannot separate our body from our emotional and spiritual well-being, as these three parts of us are so closely intertwined. Sadly, most doctors in the western world simply treat the symptoms by prescribing medication, instead of finding out the cause of the physical sickness. I do not mean to say that our emotional well-being or our character determines *all* diseases, for there are contagious diseases that are of a physical origin, and there are structural diseases, which also could be of a physical origin—for example, a broken bone. I do not have time to go into depth in this book about the emotional and mental connection to diseases. There is enough research available to prove this truth.

We have to understand the connections between right-living and physical, emotional, and spiritual well-being. Our attitudes influence our bodies in a positive or in a negative way, depending on the attitude. Many scientific tests have proven this. It has been proven that just thinking about resentment toward another person will tense the muscles of the body and release chemical toxins from the brain into the body. A counselor once said that he knows of no single thing that causes more havoc in the human body than resentments, for resentment is poison.

In Proverbs 3:5–8, we also see a direct connection between the way we live and physical health:

> *Trust in the LORD with all your heart,*
> *and lean not on your own understanding; in*
> *all your ways acknowledge Him, and He*
> *shall direct your paths. Do not be wise in*
> *your own eyes; fear the LORD and depart*

from evil. It will be health to your flesh, and
strength to your bones.

Here we are told that certain things will be health to us. What are those things? First of all, they include trust. We are told to "trust in the Lord with all our heart," which will end up bringing health to us. We were not created to live in unbelief, and we are not supposed to control our own lives and circumstances.

The opposite of trust is fear and worry. If trust brings health to our bodies, then fear and worries will take our health. The next thing we are told is to acknowledge the Lord in all our ways, meaning to put Him first in all our decisions. We were created to live in a close relationship with Him; therefore, if we live life our own way, we will be out of balance with ourselves and suffer the consequences physically.

Next, we are told not to be wise in our own eyes, which is a sign of pride and will show its effects in our health too. Pride and self-dependency are closely related and are great enemies to our physical health.

Lastly, we are told to fear the Lord and depart from evil. To fear the Lord does not mean to be afraid of Him, but to live a life of worship and surrender to Him. We must turn from our own ways and live life the way God shows us in His Word so that we can enjoy health to our bodies. Again, God is not going to curse or punish us if we don't live life God's way; the punishment has been placed on Christ. We simply suffer the consequences for not living life the smart way, which is God's way.

As you read the following statements and stories, you will realize how much our health is affected by so many things. Having said this, I want to emphasize again that I am absolutely convinced that God always wants to heal us. He neither wants us to live with sick bodies, nor with souls that are unwell. He desires for us to be totally well because He loves us and cares about us. Besides this, we have a purpose to fulfill here on this earth, which is to demonstrate His great love to all people.

A doctor was baffled over the cause of sickness in a baby. One day upon visiting the child, he came into the home while the parents were quarreling and saw the mother breastfeeding the baby during the argument. The doctor threw up his hands and said, "Now I know what the matter with your baby is; you are poisoning it by this ill will!" The poison was in the mother's milk, put there by anger. In two days the child was dead.

A missionary in China did not want the wife of the doctor to visit her when she had her baby. The knowledge of this upset the doctor's wife; there were strained relations. The flow of the mother's milk stopped two days after the child was born. The upset with the doctor's wife was responsible for the stoppage.

A doctor in the Mayo Clinic once said that he could see a stomach ulcer healing before his very eyes on the X-ray when a patient surrendered her resentments.

A pastor had his heart set on a certain appointment. When he did not get it, his wife became embittered and ill and died shortly afterward; he himself became spiritually so upset that he left the ministry. Resentment killed the body of one and the soul of the other. It was poison.

One of the outstanding doctors of a great city said: "In my clinic, we have decided that 75 percent of the people who come to us would be well if they changed their attitudes. They are throwing functional disturbances into their systems by wrong moral and spiritual attitudes."

A highly cultured lady said that when her husband began to pay attention to another woman, she broke out with eczema. Only when she surrendered the fear and worry to God did the eczema go away.

Dr. W. C. Alvarez, the stomach specialist at the Mayo Clinic, said that 80 percent of the stomach difficulties that come to them are not organic, but functional. Wrong mental and spiritual attitudes throw functional disturbance into digestion.

A lady said that she lived with her son-in-law for five years. He developed a stomach ulcer, and she developed arthritis. The tensions between them were responsible.

A girl was taken to the hospital to be operated on for intestinal difficulty. They found she was worrying over the news of her brother who was about to lose his mind. When she brought this fear up and out, she left the hospital well. The disturbance was the result of fear and worry.

A long time ago, airplanes in France provided a cup in front of each passenger with a sign, *"For airsickness."* In English planes, the notice read, *"In case you feel indisposed, the stewardess will help you."* In the English planes, scarcely anyone got sick, but in the French planes, almost everyone did! Passengers looked at the word *sickness* and the cup, and it was enough to make them sick! But when they read the sign in the English planes, they thought of a stewardess. The attention was called off of self, and the sickness was pushed to the margin.

Punishment and Consequences

It is important to understand the difference between punishment and consequences. If we believe that God is an angry God who is beating us for our sins, or even worse, for our mistakes, we will have no faith to come to Him and receive our miracles of healing. The punishment for our sin has been placed upon Christ, but all of our sins, as well as all of our choices, have consequences. We can select our choices, but we can never select the consequences of our choices.

We were not created to live in unbelief or with any negative attitude. We were created in the image of God who is love; therefore, we were created to live in love. If we do not do so, it will affect our entire being, including our health. It is not God punishing us, but we are suffering the consequences for living against the way we were created. Resentments, worries, bitterness, and unresolved emotional issues all affect our health. We must not only seek divine healing through the supernatural power of God, but always go to the roots of any issues in our lives.

If worry, for instance, causes stomach or digestive problems for you, and the anointing and power of God brings you a supernatural healing, then if you don't deal with the root and get rid of your worries, you will have the same problem again very soon. I don't believe that God punished the lady from our church with an inflamed shoulder because she held resentment against her sister. I believe that resentment poisoned her body. We were created to love and not to be resentful, so the natural consequences were that her mind and soul passed on the poison of the resentment to her body. Many physical problems also come from poisoning our bodies with foods that are very harmful for us or from being overweight and obese. Let us be smart and remove the roots of the sicknesses from our lives so that we can glorify God with our bodies.

Let us believe in and pursue divine health as well as divine healing for all those who are in need. Lay your hands on the sick and boldly command the sicknesses to disappear. It is the desire of God's heart to demonstrate His great love to the lost by healing the sick.

Testimony

My name is Elizangela, and I suffered an accident a year ago. After the accident, I could not run or bend my knees anymore because one of my knees got hurt. As I did not have medical care, after some time, the other knee was also damaged. It had inflammation and got so bad that the nerves were affected. I suffered a lot of pain for almost a year, and the doctor's diagnosis was that I could not be healed. But, today, I received prayer, and I am totally healed. I received a miracle from God.

Testimony

My ankle and knees were damaged really badly because I rode my bike very hard. At a church service, after a word of knowledge about the pain I suffered, I stood up and received some prayer for healing. The following day I noticed I was healed. I climbed and walked, and I felt no pain. I went to work, and there simply was no pain. I was healed by the power of Jesus Christ.

Testimony

My name is Giumara, I am from Brasilia, Brazil. I was married for 11 years, and I still had no children. One day, I received prayer to have my womb blessed. From that day on, I got prayer and a prophetic word that I would be pregnant. The doctors told me I could never have children naturally. I went through many tests, but God showed me who He is and that He would fulfill His promise. For His honor and glory, seven months later I was pregnant, and today my son, Isaac, is two years old. He is a blessing in my life. All glory is given to the Lord. My husband also got a word from God that he would be very prosperous. After many tests, and less than a year later, my husband has another job, and he earns much more than before that prophecy. God is good.

Chapter 21

Let's Do It

I hope that this book is not just another book that people have loved to read, but that it will also be a book that will inspire, challenge, and motivate every reader to begin to move in the supernatural. We have a mission and a commission from our Lord Jesus Christ, which is to reach the world with the Good News. This task cannot be successfully completed without the demonstration of the supernatural power of God. Let us do it and show this world that Jesus Christ is still alive, loves them, and cares for them.

Our Confession

An important part of the supernatural is the power of our words. Most people agree with me that communication is an important key to a successful relationship. Few people realize, however, that the original purpose of speaking was not communication. In heaven, we will be able to communicate from spirit to spirit without using words. We will be able to use words, but we will not have to. It will be a perfect way of communicating without any possibility of misunderstandings. Many relationships face problems because of misunderstandings regarding what has been said. If we truly want to understand the power of our words, we have to, once again, apply the law of first mention. Genesis 1:1–3 says,

> *In the beginning God created the heavens and the earth. The earth was without form, and void; and darkness was on the face of the deep. And the Spirit of God was hovering over the face of the waters. Then God said, "Let there be light"; and there was light.*

This is the first mention of speaking in the Bible. When God spoke, the purpose was not to communicate anything to anyone, but to create. Therefore, we can know that the original and primary purpose of words is not communication, but creation. When God opens His mouth and speaks, He also creates. Everything that He says comes into existence by the power of His words. Every promise He speaks is a reality in the spiritual world. The sad thing is that many of these promises remain in the spiritual world and are never brought into our natural world. This can only be done by believing and confessing these promises. God's Word, in our mouths, has the same creative power as His Word in His mouth. God's people can have what they confess, but instead they often confess what they have.

A group of scientists made an experiment with some plants. They put the same type of plants in two separate rooms with the same environment in each room. Every day they talked to the plants in one room in an affirmative and positive way, saying things like, "You are so lovely. You are growing so beautifully." They also talked to the plants in the other room in a negative way: "You are such a stupid plant. You are not even growing. You are dying." The result was that the plant to which the scientists spoke in a positive way grew while the other one died. Our words have power, for good or for evil. The reason why God's words have creative power is because they are *His words*. Anybody who declares His words can see the same results as He would when He speaks them. This is demonstrated in the life of Abraham in Romans 4:17:

> *(As it is written, "I have made you a father of many nations") in the presence of Him whom he believed—God, who gives life to the dead and calls those things which do not exist as though they did...*

God calls the things that do not exist as though they did, which means that in the spiritual world they already exist because God declared them. The moment God said to Abraham that he would have Isaac, Isaac already existed in the spiritual world. Abraham had to cooperate with God's purpose in order to bring Isaac into existence in the natural world where he lived. This had to be done by faith and confession.

God changed Abraham's name from *Abram*, which means "high or exalted father," to *Abraham*, which means "father of many." Why was that so important? Faith without confession is not enough to see the supernatural. In the following two verses, we see that God did not just change Abraham's name, but Sarah's name also (Gen. 17:5, 15):

> *No longer shall your name be called Abram, but your name shall be Abraham; for I have made you a father of many nations. . . . Then God said to Abraham, "As for Sarai your wife, you shall not call her name Sarai, but Sarah shall be her name."*

Sarai means "my princess," while *Sarah* means "mother of many nations." We must not underestimate the creative power of our words. It is a universally established law in the spiritual world that cannot be changed: our words have creative power. Look at the following scriptures, and you will see the importance of our words,

> *In the beginning was the Word, and the Word was with God, and the Word was God. He was in the beginning with God. All things were made through Him, and without Him nothing was made that was made. In Him was life, and the life was the light of men.*
>
> —JOHN 1:1–4

> *. . . who being the brightness of His glory and the express image of His person, and upholding all things by the word of His power. . .*
>
> —HEBREWS 1:3

Nothing was created without the spoken and declared Word of God, and nothing is sustained without it. If our hearts can grasp the truth of the power of the declared Word of God, we will be more careful about what we speak.

Co-Creating with God

Since God's words have creative power, we can co-create with God by believing and declaring what He says. The Bible tells us in Psalm 119:89, "Forever, O LORD, Your Word is settled in heaven." This means that when God declares anything, it is firmly established and settled in the spiritual world as an absolute truth. We do not live in the heavens but on this earth. We can bring the supernatural from heaven to this earth by cooperating with God by faith and confession. Psalm 115:16 tells us, "The heaven, even the heavens are the LORD's, but the earth He has given to the children of men." It is our responsibility to bring everything God has said and declared in the heavens down to this earth where we live.

I remember very well when we planted our first church in Austria. It was very difficult to get people saved and come to the church. Evangelical churches were considered a cult, and people were afraid to come to the services. One day, as we were praying, God spoke to us through Isaiah 43:5–6:

> *Fear not, for I am with you; I will bring your descendants from the east, and gather*

*you from the west; **I will say** to the north, "Give them up!" And to the south, "Do not keep them back!" Bring My sons from afar, and My daughters from the ends of the earth.* (Emphasis mine)

Because God said that to us, we began to declare what He declared, every day. We pointed to the north and said, "Give them up." We pointed to the south and said, "Do not keep them back. Bring my sons from afar and my daughters from the ends of the earth." As we began to do that in faith, suddenly people began to come from all the different areas of our county. They came to the meetings, got saved, and became members of our church.

What Effect Do God's Words Have?

Here are some of the effects of the Words of God. Remember, it makes no difference out of whose mouth they come, as long as they are declared in faith. We must not confess *until* we believe, but we must confess *because* we believe. God's words create, as we have already seen. We should be speaking life, health, prosperity, blessing, protection, and so forth. God's words also edify, which we see in 1 Corinthians 14:3, *"But he who prophesies speaks edification and exhortation and comfort to men."* To *prophesy* means "to speak forth what God is saying." To *edify* means to "promote someone's growth in the Christian life."

The Bible tells us that we should all prophesy. That is not something just for the prophets to do, but for every single Christian so that the whole body of Christ can be built up and edified. Every time we criticize, we grieve the Holy Spirit. Every time we speak God's words of encouragement, love, and kindness to each other, we edify the body of Christ.

Jack Hayford, a well-known American pastor of a large church, was driving his car when he witnessed another driver who almost caused a fatal accident because of his reckless driving. Jack shouted, "You idiot!" He was immediately rebuked by God who told him, "I created no one by that description." We must use the words that come out of our mouths to edify.

God's words also identify. Since the word of God gives us identity, it is important to speak what God says and not what we feel or see with our natural eyes. If the church can grasp this truth, we will experience a revolution and a radical transformation in our nations. God says that we are perfectly righteous, loved, and accepted, holy and pure. That is the identity of every child of God.

Research shows that as long as people try to *become* something or someone, they never have any self-worth. If you try to become righteous, you have no self-worth because the very fact that you are trying to become righteous means that you do not see yourself as righteous. Your self-worth is directly connected to what or who you presently believe that you are. Therefore, we have to confess who God says we are and not who we think we are. Without self-worth, we cannot fulfill God's purpose and love all men. If we are trying to become righteous, holy, loved, good Christians, we will always lack self-worth.

We *have* to *believe* what God speaks over us and agree with Him by confessing the same truths. My identity is in Christ alone and in nothing else. I am who God says I am because I am in Christ Jesus. My identity is not in my past, not in my works or achievements, and not in what people say about me. In the following scriptures, we are told that we are accepted, blessed, a new creation, righteous, and a child of God. It is God's words that give us our identity, and we must believe them and confess them:

> ...*to the praise of the glory of His grace, by which He has made us accepted in the Beloved.*
>
> —EPHESIANS 5:6

> *Blessed be the God and Father of our Lord Jesus Christ, who has blessed us with every spiritual blessing in the heavenly places in Christ* ...
>
> —EPHESIANS 1:3

> *Therefore, if anyone is in Christ, he is a new creation; old things have passed away; behold, all things have become new.*
>
> —2 CORINTHIANS 5:17

> *For He made Him who knew no sin to be sin for us, that we might become the righteousness of God in Him.*
>
> —2 CORINTHIANS 5:21

> *But as many as received Him, to them He gave the right to become children of God, to those who believe in His name.*
>
> —JOHN 1:12

Our lives are a direct result of what our hearts believe and confess. We are told in Romans 10:9–10,

> . . . *that if you* **confess with your mouth** *the Lord Jesus and* **believe in your heart** *that God has raised Him from the dead, you will be saved. For with* **the heart one believes** *unto righteousness, and* **with the mouth confession is made** *unto salvation.*
> (Emphasis mine)

When you are confronted with any situation that needs the supernatural intervention of God, you must believe in your heart and confess with your mouth in order to see the power of God released.

Experiencing the Supernatural

This book must not be just another great book that you read. It must become a life-experience so that God will be glorified through you. The reason why I have added many testimonies in this book, told by those who personally experienced these miracles, is to inspire you to a life in the supernatural.

How can you experience the supernatural on a regular basis? That is the question I hope I have answered throughout this book. As I told you at the beginning of this book, the Bible says that we should seek the Lord and His strength. Nobody can make this choice for you; you have to make it for yourself. We have to pursue a supernatural lifestyle in order to experience it.

There is a story about a young man, desperate to live a godly life. He went into the desert to talk to a hermit and ask him for advice. As he was sitting outside the tent of this hermit asking him why some men begin to pursue God but then give up, while others are not distracted until the day they die, a rabbit ran past them. The hermit's dog saw the rabbit and loudly barking, began to chase it. Soon other dogs, alerted by the barking, followed in the chase.

As the rabbit kept running zigzag, one dog after the other dropped out until the hermit's dog was the only one still chasing the rabbit. The hermit looked at his student and said, "This is the answer to your question. My dog is the only one who saw the rabbit; therefore, he is the only one who did not give up." Ask God to open your eyes so that you can see the glory of the kingdom of God expressed through His supernatural power through you. Almost 40 years ago, I saw the rabbit; therefore, I am still chasing it.

Radical Faith

Unless we decide to live a life of radical faith, the supernatural will only be a theory and remain distant to us. This decision to live a radical life of faith must affect every area of our lives. Make a choice to read, study, think, and *talk* faith. Stay away from people of unbelief if they refuse to change and want to remain in their unbelief.

We must love all people and be willing to help all people. However, if people make a choice to live a life of unbelief and want to convince us to do the same, I advise you to stay away from them. I am willing to discuss the supernatural and divine healing with anybody who is hungry for it. I am not willing to discuss this subject with people who are negative and are trying to convince me that God is not a God of the supernatural and does not do miracles today. Throughout the Gospels, we see that Jesus constantly confronted unbelief.

Get Rid of All Excuses

Do not tolerate any excuses as to why God does not want to do miracles. There is no excuse why you should not experience the supernatural. I have shown you throughout this book that God has already determined for you to experience His power. We are all walking down life's road. There is a road that surely leads to failure, which is the road filled with excuses. That road represents an excuse why you cannot succeed.

As long as you accept and tolerate excuses in your life as to why you personally cannot be a channel of the supernatural power of God, you will surely follow this wrong road and never experience the power of God in your life. These excuses can be countless, such as, *"I am not spiritual enough"*; *"I am not in full-time ministry"*; *"I have failed before"*; *"I am just an ordinary person"*; *"I am not worthy"*; and many more like them.

When I began to pray for the sick, determined to see the power of God flow through me, I experienced many setbacks. The first few people I prayed for got worse instead of better. People criticized and rejected me for being radical. I was determined not to accept any excuses as to why the power of God should not be manifested through me.

Gifts and Character

Gifts and character must go hand-in-hand in our lives. Some people want nothing but character and never see the supernatural power of God in their lives. Others passionately pursue gifts, yet lack character and often end up destroyed because of it. We don't need one or the other; we must have *both* of them equally in our lives. Gifts are given to us by God, while character is developed by us. In the Old Testament, Samson had the gift but lacked character, which in the end destroyed his life. We are told in Galatians 5:6 that faith works through love: *"For in Christ Jesus neither circumcision nor uncircumcision avails anything, but faith working through love."* Faith is a gift given to us from God; walking in love is an aspect of character that has to be developed by us.

Follow Jesus, Not Men

There is a great danger as we pursue a supernatural lifestyle to follow men instead of following Christ. This has repeated itself throughout ancient and modern church history. As different men and women have learned to tap into the supernatural power of God, they were idolized by others who followed them instead of Jesus. This is something that we must avoid at all costs because it greatly grieves our Lord Jesus Christ. Jesus told His apostles to preach the gospel and make disciples. He never wanted them to make their own disciples, but disciples of Jesus. Matthew 28:19–20 says,

> *Go therefore and make disciples of all the nations, baptizing them in the name of the Father and of the Son and of the Holy Spirit,* **teaching them to observe all things that I have commanded you;** *and lo, I am with you always, even to the end of the age. Amen.* (Emphasis mine)

Jesus said to "teach them all that I have commanded you." I believe in discipleship. God, in His grace, has given me disciples in different countries of the world. My goal is for them to follow Christ passionately and not to follow me. That is true discipleship. Don't follow man; follow Jesus with all of your heart.

This week I received a message from a lady in São Paulo. She told me that her niece had been sick for several days with a high fever. Nothing helped nor removed the fever from that child. She asked me to pray for her niece for a miracle. I responded that I would not pray for her niece because she has the same authority that I do. I told her to go to her niece, lay her hands on her, rebuke every spirit of infirmity, and command it to leave the body. I told her to command the fever to be gone. Probably about two hours later, I received an exciting message from her telling me that her niece was fever-free because she did what I told her to do. I did not refuse to pray for her niece because I did not care, but because I am determined to see the body of Christ mobilized to walk in the supernatural.

Thank you, from all of my heart, for reading this book. It is my prayer that this book will release a hunger and desperation in your heart to be a channel of the supernatural power of God. If this book has achieved that purpose, please share it with others.

Testimony

I am from Catalão, Brazil. For five years I couldn't hear with my right ear. After receiving prayer, I was healed. Today, I can hear perfectly with my right ear.

Testimony

My name is Naiara; I live in Catalão, Brazil. I had a paralyzed hand. After a church meeting, I received some prayer, and my hand got healed. I can move my fingers again. Everything is normal.

Made in the USA
Middletown, DE
24 December 2016